ENJOY THE JOURNEY

CHANGE YOUR PARADIGM...
... CHANGE YOUR DESTINY!

ENJOY THE JOURNEY

CHANGE YOUR PARADIGM. . .
. . . CHANGE YOUR DESTINY!

CREATED FOR THE 99% OF PEOPLE WHO ARE LOST, BROKEN, AND SEEKING PURPOSE AND JOY IN LIFE

David E. VanEpps

Published by

Enjoy the Journey, LLC

38807 Harper Ave

Clinton Township, MI 48036

ISBN: 978-0-9973778-7-3

Library of Congress Control Number: 2016917789

VanEpps, David E.

Enjoy the Journey, Change Your Paradigm... Change Your Destiny

Printed in the United States of America

Cover design: Vanessa Mendozzi

Book layout and design: Slaven Kovacevic

Permissions:

Getting Things Done® and the GTD® system are registered trademarks of the David Allen Company.

Used with full permission of the David Allen Company

For more information, visit www.gettingthingsdone.com

"Secrets to Success" by Eric Thomas

Used with full permission of Eric Thomas and Associates, LLC

For more information, visit www.ETinspires.com

Ironman® is a registered trademark of World Triathlon Corporation ("WTC"). An Ironman® triathlon is part of a series of long-distance triathlon races that are coordinated by the WTC. Usage of the Ironman® trademark in this publication refers specifically to an Ironman distance triathlon and/or a person who has completed an Ironman® triathlon.

For more information, visit www.Ironman.com

P90X® is a registered trademark of Beachbody, LLC.

For more information, visit www.beachbody.com

PRAISE FOR
ENJOY THE JOURNEY

"Dave has gone from being an overweight, middle-aged guy to an elite athlete. He has an incredible attitude, and Enjoy the Journey *will help you develop a positive mindset and the qualities of success that will change your world forever."*

~Jeff Wald, co-owner of Jeff & Kina Wald Fitness, Portland, TN

*"*Enjoy the Journey *is incredibly inspiring in every way! I felt challenged mentally, motivated physically, and encouraged spiritually. You will love this book!"*

~Chris Zarbaugh, Pastor, Kensington Community Church

"Dave knows firsthand what it takes to make a complete transformation occur in every aspect mind, body and spirit. Enjoy the Journey *is very inspirational and will help others transform their lives as well!"*

~Cindy Crandell, Functional Medicine R.N., Nuview Nutrition

"This is not a textbook... but a conversation with the most important person in your life—you! Dave continues to walk the walk while providing strategies to address how one can enrich their purpose in life."
~Kevin Thompson, Vocational and Youth Sports Coach, Webster, NY

"In this book David tells some stories about people that have faced some very difficult, even tragic, events in their lives and turned them around to be amazing events that uplifted their life to a higher plane. I have read stories and books like that before. Those people were not me. Enjoy the Journey *spoke to me more profoundly than that because the most amazing story in the book is Dave's own story. He took an already good life and transformed his outlook to take ownership of that life to make it even better. To make it amazing. That story, the motivation and the process behind it, is more than worth a read. It is worth emulating. Thank you, Dave, for your story and your detailed advice."*
~Alan Willett | President, Oxseeker Inc., http://oxseeker.net/ Author of *Leading the Unleadable*, Ithaca, NY

"I have known Dave as a friend and colleague for over twenty years. He is one of the most genuine and positive individuals I have ever met. In Enjoy the Journey *he connects his life experiences as an Ironman, business executive, paramedic and missionary in ways that are moving, heartwarming and inspirational. Dave's enthusiasm is contagious, and his story reveals powerful messages about confidence, commitment, and gratitude."*
~Fred Damiano, Chief Information Officer, Rochester, NY

"I've known Dave since Cub Scouts, he has always challenged himself to improve his mind, heart and soul. That's what Enjoy the Journey *will do for you! You'll want more of it! When in his presence, he always wants you to enjoy some of that warmth in his heart that he is feeling too.* Enjoy the Journey *will do that and more!"*
~Craig Modern, High School Lacrosse Coach, Webster, NY

"Enjoy the Journey *is a captivating book for all types... VanEpps' life experiences shape this book to pursue your wildest dreams, believing that everything is possible."*
~Alex Calder, Director of Development, Kensington Community Church

"Dave has a calm and yet incredibly dynamic spirit, always a kind word of support and a great reliance on our Creator in his life. I have found him to be an inspiration as an Ironman teammate and as a friend."
~Paul Mozak, Vice President Finance and Chief Risk Officer, Blue Cross Blue Shield of Michigan

"Dave was one of my biggest warriors during one of the most difficult times in my life... It inspired me and gave me hope, when at times, I didn't think there was any."
~Angie Pennington, Owner, insPire-works

"There simply could not be a more appropriate title for a book written by Dave than Enjoy the Journey. *His fine leadership, and friendship offered through that leadership, affords you the opportunity to witness his inspiring life journey, and more importantly the opportunity to reflect more honestly on your own personal journey. In reading this book you will learn things of goodness, patience, giving, humor, grace, vision and intelligence. I highly recommend reading this book so you can enjoy and share so many of the same stories I have heard, remembered, and passed along over my years of knowing Dave. So, enjoy the read and enjoy the journey!"*

~Lisa Rennell, Marketing Professional, Detroit, MI

"Dave is a leader that you would follow into battle. He has the moral compass and direction to a God-given life. His compassion drives you to become more than you ever thought you could be."

~Susan Smith, Ironman Swim Coach, Detroit, MI

"Dave has been an awesome example of Christian leadership! ...So many questions as I grow in my Christian life. Dave has been able to take situations and pull out examples in the Bible to relate them to my work life/family life."

~Julie Stelzner, Information Technology Professional, Downers Grove, IL

"I have been fortunate to count Dave VanEpps as a teammate in both 2015 and 2016. During our countless hours together running and biking, Dave's stories and experiences have helped me immensely on my journey to become a better athlete and a better

man. He has the uncanny ability to put that which seems impossibly difficult into perspective. I could go on. He is an amazing teammate and mentor. I often think to myself, 'What would Dave do?' The answer to that question has yet to steer me wrong."
~George Harris, Triathlete and
Ultra-Marathoner, Detroit, MI

"I first met Dave VanEpps on a mission trip to Haiti. We've taken two trips together. What first stood out to me was the incredible servant's heart he has for others. His incredible servant's heart comes through in this book. Dave is a very practical, down-to-earth guy. He is inspiring to people of any age or vocation. Dave gives you a step-by-step approach, a blueprint to living the life God has called you to live. A life of joy with the time you still have here. Dave shows you that the real heroes are the ones who humble themselves enough to live a life for others. In turn, they reach their goals too."
~Tim Morton, High School Teacher and
Basketball Coach, Rochester Hills, MI

"Dave absolutely lives, breathes and sleeps the 'glass is half full' mantra. You cannot help but be inspired by this guy's words and actions."
~Robert Moore, Corporate Vice
President, Rochester, NY

"Dave is one of the most driven and inspired individuals I have ever had the pleasure to work with. His extraordinary journey is one for the books. It will help anyone with his or her own personal development and growth in an inspiring, passionate, life-fulfilling kind of way."
~Carly Secoy, Dietitian at Nuview
Nutrition, Clarkston, MI

ACKNOWLEDGMENTS

IN MY DAYS OF BEING a paramedic, people used to hear the stories and tell me that I should write a book. I didn't take it seriously, as the idea of writing solely about the misfortunes of others didn't appeal to me. After completing Ironman, people heard the stories and said I should write a book. Over the course of many Town Hall meetings with my team at work, when I would often speak words of encouragement, empowerment, and inspiration, I've been told I should write a book. I never really believed I could do it.

My friend Camille Norton retired from Acxiom several years ago, and when she did, she made me promise her one thing. She said, *"Dave, I've been so inspired and learned so much from you that's not only helped me in the workplace, but it's transferred to all areas of my life. The reason I'm able to retire now is because you helped me set this as a goal. Someday, when you write a book, promise me you'll give me a signed copy."* She didn't say if, she said when. I promised. I wondered why she believed in me so strongly when I wasn't really convinced. Much like the rest of this book, her words sank in, and I eventually believed in myself. And yes, Camille, your signed copy is on the way...

After completing Ironman, I realized my life's stories had the ability to transform minds, hearts, and lives. Unfortunately, I didn't know where to start or how to go about writing and publishing a book. I heeded the advice found in this book, and I stood on the shoulders of giants.

My wife, Charlotte, got me connected with a course at Macomb Community College called "*How to Write a Book in 30 Days.*" This is where I met author, speaker, life coach, and writing coach Don Staley. Not only is Don a fantastic coach, he's truly an incredible person who lives a powerfully inspiring life.

This book wouldn't be possible without the never-ending love of my Lord and Savior, Jesus Christ. After spending years running from him, in fear of how He might perceive me, and completely convinced He could never love me, I finally dropped to my knees. With the power of the message one morning at Kensington Community Church, my paradigm shifted. I realized that I'm broken, you're broken, and we're all broken. Yet God still loves us—just the way we are. He wants to meet us in our brokenness, where we are, and help us through our difficulties. Without this faith, I realize my life, my hope, and my joy would be so much less, and I never would have fulfilled my destiny.

A special thank you to my incredible wife, Charlotte. Aside from Jesus Christ, you are my North Star. You show unconditional love, and your support is unbelievable—you don't just support me, you encourage me, cheer me on, and you're with me every step of the way. When I fall, you pick me back up. You've also slowed me down so that I take more time to truly enjoy our life together rather than burning the candle at both ends all the time. I've never known anyone who could handle stress the way you do. You truly don't sweat the small stuff, and you are an amazing role model for women—calm, confident, strong, loving, and you can always put situations in perspective. Not to mention, you're a major reason why I truly do enjoy the journey of life. I'm pretty sure we say it at least once a day to each other, "Life, with you, is awesome…"

My daughter Tori… you're amazing—so smart, talented, successful, and capable. There's nothing you can't do! You have already achieved a lot in your young life, and you continue to show amazing potential. You have the mindset for winning, and you know how to get it done. You're also wired a lot like me, so make sure you slow down enough to enjoy life. Doing life with you for 21 years has been a huge inspiration in writing this book.

My daughter Lexi... you are an unbelievable young woman who is already changing the world. Your purpose and priorities are crystal clear, and you're already a role model at having fun and enjoying the journey of life. You've proven over and over that when you set your mind to something, you're unstoppable. Be confident in who you are, knowing that true approval comes from above and within. As you can imagine, your never-ending joy has been immensely inspirational in the writing of this book.

My stepdaughter, Natalie... you have so much potential and opportunity ahead of you, and you really can have it all. Entering college, you're facing so many decisions about who you are and what your life is all about. You've already demonstrated that the sky's the limit as you've excelled in school, music, and life. Be true to who you are, keep loving life, and you will have an abundance of success and happiness in life.

My stepson, Danny... just a few years ago you learned to skate, and now you're a fantastic hockey player. In those few years you've improved in all aspects of your life and gained confidence in who you are. Keep believing in yourself, keep working hard, and keep focused on your passions, and you will have an amazingly successful life. You know how to laugh, you know how to make others laugh, and as you go through high school and beyond, as you find your purpose and direction, you will truly be unstoppable.

My parents, Ed and Pauline VanEpps... you're some of the most amazing people on the planet. You've always been loving and supportive; your life is a reflection of what you teach. You gave me the right tools in life to be successful, you've encouraged me every step of the way, and you've always spoken life into me. You've also taught me to be present, engaged, and joyful. In fact, at least once a week I'm pretty sure you ask me if I'm taking time to relax and enjoy myself amidst the whirlwind. Throughout life, I always remember you walking the talk. You taught me, you coached me, and you modeled the behaviors you expected of me. Your unconditional love, especially through my teenage years, has been a great example of what our Heavenly Father's love looks like for his children. I could dedicate books to you, but I could never thank you enough.

My in-laws, Dan and Barb Young... you're truly amazing people. Many of the positive words spoken in this book are things I hear you speak into your children and grandchildren each and every day. Positive, inspirational, motivational, loving, and uplifting. Your unconditional love has been evident from the day I met you, and your support has been amazing. Even when you didn't fully understand much about my racing, I remember you coming to my first major bike race, cheering me on, and then being so excited that you drove the 130-mile course the next day. What I'll always cherish is that you weren't excited about a race—you were excited because it was important to me. You certainly walk the talk when it comes to speaking life, speaking truth, and being positive role models.

Denise VanEpps... you're a world-class sister, world-class physical therapist, and miracle worker. We've been through every high and low that life's thrown at us, and you continue to inspire me each and every day. I couldn't have asked for a better sister to grow up with! My brother-in-law, Jeff Moriarty... great physical therapist, great athlete, gutsy mountain climber, and all around fantastic guy. Thanks for sharing the journey of life with us...

Gordie and Val Young, Maddie, Nolan, and Lindsey. I love you very much and will always be grateful for the love, support, and fun times we continue to share. Physically you are miles away, but in reality you're always in my mind and heart. Your unconditional love, along with sharing our spiritual journeys in small group, has helped shape and inspire my life's story.

Nuview Nutrition—Carly Secoy and Terri Caunt. The two greatest nutritionists in the world, as voted by me. I came to you reluctantly, as I was afraid to ask for help. I was a train wreck, and I presented you a monumental challenge. You took the facts, worked with me, set the goals, set the action plan, held me accountable, and then monitored and tweaked the plan along the way. Without you I would likely be struggling with life-threatening health issues instead of enjoying the journey. You made a difference and inspired me in the process.

Dr. Paz—your honesty set everything in motion. When you first said I had high blood pressure and needed to lose weight, I told you I was exercising and eating right. I thought I was, but I wasn't. You gave me one chance, but the second time I tried to use that line on you, you called me on the carpet. You didn't accept my excuse, and you called me to action right away. If you hadn't, I'd probably be dead by now. Seriously.

Coach John, I may never know what you saw in me in the first place—couldn't swim, couldn't run, and yet you believed I could be an Ironman within a year. I'm grateful you believed, and I'm grateful that you made me physically and mentally tough enough to rise to the challenge.

To my JY-Tri (www.JY-Tri.com) teammates, this wouldn't be possible without seeing your smiling faces every morning at 5:30 a.m. How ironic that some of life's most powerful lessons came when we hadn't yet showered and smelled like sweat. But it doesn't matter. We put it all out on the line, and together we accomplish more by 7 a.m. every day than most people do in an entire week. We've laughed, we've cried, we've struggled, and we've succeeded. Jason Grembi—you're possibly the most athletic person I've ever met and I'm truly humbled by how amazing you are at all three disciplines. Andrea Kuhn—you're an amazing teammate, a hard worker, and you're a prime example of what someone can do when they believe in themselves and work at it. Amy Beaulac—you're a better athlete than you will ever realize, and you have so much to offer in this sport and in life. Your passion and joy is evident in all that you do. As you continue to believe, you will continue to achieve. Steve Martin—you're a true brother, an amazing teammate, an outstanding family man, an unbelievable athlete, and as a person you rise to the cream of the crop. You're a class act and a wonderful friend. George Harris—you may be the best natural athlete, yet you're the most humble. You redefine the word *teammate* and radiate an aura of kindness, compassion, and friendship everywhere you go. Paul Mozak—you're the silent hero of this group. You've talked me off the ledge several times, and you're one of the most inspiring, humble leaders who exudes class in all that you do. If more young men role modeled their lives after you, this world would be a better place. Susan Smith—you're a miracle worker in the pool, and I will forever be grateful for your coaching and inspiration. I can't believe what you've done to improve my swim in such a short time, and your winning attitude helps raise the bar of excellence. Christina and Ted—you're on the same journey I was last year. Stay focused, stay strong, and great things will happen!

Barbara Turner—you're a role model when it comes to turning lemons into lemonade. Injuries may have stopped your triathlon training, so you turned to running. You rose above, and your faith continues to inspire athletic and business success. Carl Evans—my first marathon coach. You also saw something in me that I couldn't see, and your persistence won me over to the sport of running and shaped my destiny. Lastly, Janice Gallagher from DMC Physical Therapy. I walked in two weeks before Ironman with three different structural knee issues, and you worked tirelessly to heal me. Nobody thought I had a chance, but you believed in me the whole time and made it happen!

Jeff and Kina Wald—as my Team Beachbody coaches, you inspired, coached, and led me through the first legs of the journey. You taught me everything about positive accountability. Through our Facebook group, you've coached our team to train, to learn, to grow, and to become better— not only as athletes but as people. You've also created a community in which we hold each other accountable and are all positive forces working together to support each other. You exemplify Christian leadership.

Alan Willett—consultant, mentor, coach, leader, and friend. You live an amazing life that evokes curiosity, and if everyone went through life with half as much joy as you have, the world would be a better place. I've never met anyone like you—you are the master when it comes to personal and professional leadership.

Many, many friends and co-workers throughout my life have inspired me. Bob Moore, you're the most charismatic leader I know, and you naturally bring out the best in everyone. You are a role model in life. Fred Damiano, you're still my role model and the benchmark when it comes to inspirational, quality leadership. You set the bar for business leaders everywhere. Kevin Thompson and Craig Modern, my life wouldn't have been what it is without your love and friendship each and every day. You're the most amazing friends anyone could ask for. We've certainly lived together through the ups and downs, and your personal stories are never-ending sources of inspiration. Sue Schneider, you have one of the biggest hearts and most generous spirits I've seen. There's nothing you won't do for friends and loved ones, and you certainly live a life that exemplifies service, character, and class. Team Acxiom, you're the most amazing team of people ever. I'm inspired by you, and I'm a better person because of the opportunity to spend each and every workday with you. As a team you demonstrate the utmost professionalism, diligence, resilience, and an unparalleled can-do attitude each and every day.

Dave Wilson, you spoke words of truth that opened my mind, my heart, and my soul. You made me realize that I'm loved unconditionally by the Father, and you set the framework that would change my life. Chris Zarbaugh, you became an instant mentor and friend. You change lives each and every day, and I couldn't be more excited to be on mission with you. The best is yet to come—we will continue to change minds, hearts, lives, and eternities! Lastly, to my brothers and sisters in Haiti, especially Samuel Cineus, you taught me about what's truly important in life. I'm forever grateful.

TABLE OF CONTENTS

INTRODUCTION

"Most of all, enjoy every moment of the journey, and appreciate where you are at this moment"

~M. Hale

CONFIRMED SHOOTING AT HUDSON AND *Avenue D. Believed to be three patients at this time...*" was the dispatcher's call. We were between calls, sitting just a few blocks away, so we were easily the first ambulance on-scene. Yes, there were three patients with gunshot wounds. First patient—shot in the head and clearly dead. Second patient—shot in the side of the lower leg—poor aim. This patient was going to be okay. Third patient—shot in the chest. This patient was our priority. Thankfully, he was conscious and alert. However, as we cut his shirt to examine the wound, I realized the worst. He had been shot three times, all in the heart. Sadly, he was dead, he just didn't know it yet. We started working aggressively, but in a matter of about two minutes, his severely damaged heart couldn't keep up. He deteriorated and died. Right before dying, amongst a few other choice words, he said, "*I can't believe it. Life is short...*"

LIFE IS TOO SHORT TO MISS

What do the following words have in common: paramedic, firefighter, executive, marathoner, missionary, Ironman, husband, father? Normally, I'd say very little.

All can be associated with stress, some can be considered borderline insane, but all of them make up my life's story. I've been blessed with some amazing experiences across a diverse set of jobs, careers, hobbies, and roles. Experiences that have inspired and motivated me, experiences that have made me laugh, and experiences that have made me cry. Experiences that showed me many wealthy people who were miserable while their dirt-poor counterparts were overflowing with joy. Experiences that showed me how busy people effectively get things done while managing stress, and others struggle with everyday life. Throughout the process, I've learned to love life, love people, and take time out to truly enjoy all that life has to offer.

In the course of these ventures, I've studied life. I've studied people. I've studied high-performing, joyful people, as well as their less-successful, unhappy counterparts. Make no mistake, there are common attributes of successful, happy people that can be broken down into mindsets and behaviors. In this book, I will share with you common mindsets of successful, happy people—those fundamental beliefs and attitudes that are prerequisite to success and happiness. I will also share with you their common behaviors—the structures you can put in place and the actions you can take to empower YOU to live the life of excellence and happiness that YOU were meant to live.

TOO MANY OF US RUSH THROUGH LIFE, GOING THROUGH THE MOTIONS

In many countries, where people identify themselves primarily with their job, people say, *"Thank God it's Monday."* In America, one of our favorite expressions is *"Thank God it's Friday."* I like to wake up and say, *"Thank God it's today."*

We are so focused on where we're going. Little kids want to grow up. High school students can't wait for college. College students can't wait to hit the workforce. People early in their careers can't wait to achieve success. People late in their careers can't wait to retire. It's human nature to wish our lives away.

While it's great to look forward with anticipation, we need to remember that life's not just about the destination, it's about the journey. So rather than wish our lives away in search of an ultimate destination, take time to enjoy the journey.

"Bloom where you're planted"
~Mary Engelbreit

In 2010, I started an amazing, incredible, fun journey—my health and fitness journey. I started out overweight with high blood pressure, high triglycerides, high cholesterol, high sugar, and in the high-risk category for heart disease. Thankfully my doctor finally looked me in the eye and gave me life-transforming advice. He didn't mince words. He very clearly told me that I was overweight, I was a high risk for heart attack, and I needed to take action, immediately. While still in his office, he told me he was stepping out for a few minutes and that I needed to "*call Tony.*" He meant that I needed to call Team Beachbody and buy Tony Horton's P90X program. It was the best first step of my life. P90X eventually led me to a number of other Team Beachbody programs, which in turn led me to become part of an Ironman training team. In parallel, I was also guided to an incredible team of nutritionists at Nuview Nutrition. My new healthy eating lifestyle combined with my exercise regimen produced amazing results: 50-pound weight loss, over 300 point reduction in triglyceride levels, over 50 point reduction in cholesterol, a reduction of 13 points on both my systolic and diastolic blood pressure, and I'm no longer in the high-risk category for cardiovascular disease. My doctor considers me to be healthy in all aspects.

DON'T TRY TO EAT AN ELEPHANT IN ONE BITE— JUST TAKE IT ONE BITE AT A TIME

In 2010, I also started another amazing, incredible, fun, and stressful journey—my spiritual journey. This journey started at a time when I was spiritually bankrupt.

I believed that there was a God, but I didn't know him at all. My life's priorities were about my family and then me, but few others. In fact, when the earthquake hit Haiti in January 2010, it didn't impact me very much at all—out of sight, out of mind. Sad, but true. Little did I know that the Haitians would soon become some of my best and closest friends on earth. I certainly wasn't the type of person who was making a lasting difference in the world, I wasn't fulfilling my destiny, and I certainly wasn't creating the best possible legacy for my children and their children.

That changed. My spiritual journey has been a journey that led me to several mission trips in Haiti, which is where I quickly became close friends with some of the most amazing people in the world. It's led me to exhilarating and exhausting service projects, amazingly deep friendships, life-transforming changes, a completely new paradigm about my purpose and outlook in life, and the opportunity to positively impact the lives of those around me. It's been fun, it's been crazy, and it's led to experiences I never would have otherwise enjoyed.

LIVING AMONGST THE POOREST OF POOR, I REALIZED THAT TRUE HAPPINESS AND JOY COME FROM WITHIN

Throughout my experiences, I've seen people at their best... and their worst. I've seen people with wealth, and I've spent time amongst the poorest of poor. One thing continues to resonate with me. Some of the happiest people I've ever met are those living in the worst of conditions—sheer poverty, minimal food, no clean water, minimal education, poor sanitation, poor health care, and zero material wealth. Yet these people are amongst the most joyful, happy, loving people I've ever met. Through these beautiful people, I learned that joy is a choice. Your attitude is a choice. Regardless of your degrees, job title, salary, athletic ability, bank account, or any other traditional western culture indicator of success, living with joy is your choice.

LIVE AN ABUNDANT LIFE AMIDST LIFE'S NEVER-ENDING CHALLENGES

My goal in writing this book is to motivate and inspire you to achieve greatness while enjoying the process. To break all self-limiting paradigms. To motivate and equip you to step out of your comfort zone. To ground you in your purpose, priorities, and goals. To help you organize yourself for excellence. To live the life of joy and excellence YOU were meant to live.

This book is not going to provide training plans or meal plans to achieve the results I've experienced. I'm not a coach, I'm not a nutritionist, and I'm certainly not qualified to teach you how to do either one. However, if any of these are important to you, this book will help you get the right mindset for success, and it will encourage you to seek the help of qualified professionals (coach, nutritionist, etc.). Ultimately, this book will set the stage for you to succeed in whatever endeavors you wish.

Let me also add that there are a number of stories in here from all domains of my life: paramedic, firefighter, executive, marathoner, missionary, Ironman, husband, and father. Any stories from my days as a paramedic or firefighter that involve patients have been edited to fully protect patient confidentiality.

Throughout the book, I've created a series of challenges to help you along your journey. These exercises are designed to help you apply the learnings to your own life. For your convenience, I've added pages to Appendix B—Challenge Journal, in which you can complete these challenges. If you have the book in electronic format, the Challenge Journal is also available for download at www.DaveVanEpps.com. If you prefer, feel free to use your own paper, electronic journal, or notebook to complete the exercises.

Let's do this!

Dave

SECTION 1

SETTING THE STAGE

CHAPTER 1

ONE IN A MILLION

You're not one in a million
—you're one in over 7.2 billion!

Do you believe that you're one in a million? Well, you should! But you shouldn't. If you were ONLY one in a million, there would be approximately 7,200 exact replicas of you walking around the earth right now! And that's clearly not the case.

It's better than being one in a million. You're one in over 7.2 billion! In fact, since the beginning of time, there has never been a person quite like you, there currently isn't another person quite like you, and there never will be another person quite like you. Nobody can think the things you think, dream the things you dream, feel the things you feel, relate to others the way you relate, and do the things you do.

Indeed, you are unique. But sadly, most people never realize this. They never realize their potential. They never realize their gifts. They never realize their unique qualities that make them different in only the greatest of ways.

But not you. The very fact that you're reading this says that you don't just want more, you crave more. You aren't satisfied with the status quo. You reject mediocrity. You realize that life's not just about the destination, it's also about the journey.

It's time to act. Most of us spend our lives waiting for someday. Someday I'll travel the world. Someday I'll start an exercise program. Someday I'll start my diet. Guess what... Someday doesn't exist! Make today your someday.

Your power lies in today, right here, right now. It's time to define the new you. It's time to declare what's rightfully yours—your destiny, your legacy for generations to come... It's time to create a roadmap and some guidelines to get there. It's time to change the world, one action at a time. Let's start with right here, right now. It's time.

> *"The wealthiest place in the world is the cemetery... there is buried the greatest treasure of untapped potential"*
>
> ~Myles Munroe

Don't let your potential go to the grave. You were born of the seeds of greatness; you were carefully architected with perfection and designed for accomplishment. You were built to fulfill destinies far greater than yourself, far greater than your self-perceived limits, and far greater than most humans ever imagine possible. You were designed to take chances, to live life, to take risks, and to make a difference. Live life to the fullest. *Carpe diem...* And just go for it. I promise you the journey of a lifetime that you won't regret.

My Challenge to You

Take just five minutes and think about the following. If you'd like to write down your answers, you can do this in Appendix B—Challenge Journal. Or just use your own notebook, or perhaps do it electronically.

» What makes you unique?
» What are your unique physical, mental, and emotional attributes?
» What are your dreams, your thoughts, your hopes?
» What untapped potential exists inside you? Where could you possibly become great and create a legacy?
» What are some of the things you are passionate about?
» How would you like to spend your time, your talent, and your treasure?
» To what destiny do you believe you were called?

CHAPTER 2

LIFE'S A JOURNEY

Life's a journey, enjoy it

W E RACED DOWN THE STREET at what seemed like 80 mph, and quite honestly it probably was at least 80. The call for a man down with his heart racing left my partner and me expecting one of two extremes. Most likely another cocaine overdose, or the worst-case scenario—a true life-threatening cardiac emergency. We weaved in and out of traffic, lights and sirens going, and as we arrived on the scene this cold October night, we were greeted by frantic family members. *"Hurry up. It's really bad. This time we don't think he's going to make it."* Yep, it had to be another cocaine overdose... Until I asked, "Why don't you think he'll make it?" They nervously exclaimed, *"He's awaiting a heart transplant, and we've never seen him quite this bad!"* Sometimes experience and intuition give you that gut feeling that things aren't quite right. This was one of those times.

Inside the house, the 27-year-old male was lying on the kitchen floor, white as snow, sweating profusely, and he had the look of death about him. I introduced myself, and all he said was, "*Please hurry, I think this is it.*" As I interviewed him and confirmed his history of degenerative cardiac disease, the supporting cast of firefighters and EMTs grabbed his vital signs and helped hook him up to the EKG. Blood pressure 90/60, heart rate 186. Not good. We broke out the drug box and drew up the drugs to address the heart rate. Then his eyes rolled back, his blood pressure bottomed out to 0/0, and his heart rate went over 220. Clinically, he wasn't pumping any oxygen to his vital organs, including his brain, and death was imminent.

We changed our course of treatment from drug therapy to shock therapy. As a quick aside, there is no treatment on the planet worse than synchronized cardioversion. It's not quite the same as the shock given when someone is in full cardiac arrest, but it's close. This type of shock has caused 95-year-old ladies to swing at me while cursing like sailors. It hurts. Nonetheless, I shocked him. Much to my pleasant surprise, he awoke immediately and his vital signs returned to normal. Even better, he didn't wake up swinging or swearing. But the real surprise was yet to come.

We packaged for transport to the hospital, and we began the trip. After some awkward silence, he looked at me and said, "*Can I tell you something really weird?*" Hey, I'm always up for a story. Bring it. I had no idea what kind of story I was about to hear. He proceeded to explain that he watched me work from above the room. While I externally acknowledged what he said, internally my brain was telling my immature mind that this was a bunch of crap. Until he proceeded to explain my every move, with precision, and from the vantage point of being on the ceiling. Pretty impressive for someone whose eyes were rolled back in his head, thereby making it physically impossible to see anything. And then he told me exactly which drawer of the drug box I reached into, what color needle I grabbed, and what numbers I pushed on my cell phone as I was calling to get a doctor's order to push the drug. Impossible. Or was it?

He described a beautiful tunnel of bright white light above him, a feeling of indescribable love and peace, and a feeling that he was being pulled into another place. And then when I delivered the shock, he felt his "being" come right back into his body. He stopped his story there, although there was clearly more. As we arrived at the hospital and transferred his care over to hospital staff, I knew he was going to be okay for now. He was still in need of his heart transplant, but for now, he was okay. I'm not sure I was. I didn't talk about this for years.

Questions started going through my mind. What else is out there that our senses cannot detect? What exists beyond life as we know it? Why are we here? What is our purpose? How should any of these answers shape how we live?

I didn't know any of these answers, but I knew one thing for sure. There's a lot more to life than we, as mere mortals, can see, feel, and hear. There's a higher purpose. There's something beyond. Something calling. Something guiding. I certainly didn't have all the answers, but I did realize one thing from this experience, as well my entire EMS career. Life's a journey. We never know how short or long it will be. But no matter what, life's a journey that was meant to be enjoyed.

And that's where the pursuit begins.

My Challenge to You

Take just five minutes and think about the following. If you'd like to write down your answers, you can do this in Appendix B—Challenge Journal. Or just use your own notebook, or perhaps do it electronically. Regardless of how you do it, just do it.

» Have you ever considered why you were put on earth?
» Do you believe that there are things we cannot perceive with our human senses?
» What exists beyond life as we know it?
» Do you believe there's more to life than just going through the daily grind?
» Are you always focused on the destination, or do you view each and every day of your life as part of a journey?
» Do you believe you have a destiny to fulfill?
» What legacy do you want to leave for generations to come?

SECTION 2

THE MINDSET

CHAPTER 3

BELIEVE IN MIRACLES

"Do you believe in miracles?"

~Al Michaels

IN 1980 THE US OLYMPIC men's hockey team was playing in the semi-final round against the undefeated, formidable, seemingly unbeatable Russian team. Coach Herb Brooks addressed the team before the game with a historic speech.

In his pre-game speech, Brooks changed minds and changed hearts. He challenged a bunch of kids who had already said, "We can't." Brooks, in his speech, said, "*If we played them 10 times they might win 9. But not tonight. NOT tonight. Tonight, we skate with them. We skate with them and we shut them down because WE CAN!*"

This dejected group of kids had already come to terms with their inevitable fate of losing. But in that instant, this group of kids had their paradigm changed, and they suddenly believed in themselves. They walked out of the locker room as winners, they played the game as winners, and as the final seconds ticked off the clock, they emerged as winners. The world was in shock. The impossible had happened. And the sportscaster Al Michaels' words will live in my head forever as he shouted to the world, "*DO YOU BELIEVE IN MIRACLES!?!?!*"

I relive the Miracle on Ice every time I visit the Olympic training center in Lake Placid. Do you believe in miracles? Those words resonate with every American who was old enough to watch TV on that evening in 1980. We're surrounded by miracles. Each and every day is a miracle. Life is a miracle. Our bodies are miracles. Things happening around us each and every day are miracles. Yet in the hustle and bustle of school, work, soccer games, Facebook updates, emails, texts, and every other distraction, we're just too busy to see them.

On one of my mission trips to Haiti, where there were no cell phones, no televisions, no electronic toys, we were asked to think about miracles. It was amazing how much more we noticed in the ensuing days. Miracles were everywhere. We were dumbfounded—how could this be possible? Why don't we see these same miracles when we're at home? Simple: we're too busy to look around.

DO YOU BELIEVE IN MIRACLES?

There's a Bible story about an epic battle between David and Goliath several thousand years ago. A battle was to take place, and David wasn't even invited. His job was to stay back and tend the sheep. But he showed up, and when nobody stepped up to take on the mighty Goliath, David rose to the occasion. David was the underdog, the kid, the shepherd, the guy with no armor. His only weapon was a slingshot. Goliath was a killing machine. A one-man wrecking crew with armor, the best weaponry, and a history of destroying everything in his path.

Everyone knew who was going to win this battle. If it occurred in modern times, Las Vegas oddsmakers wouldn't have anyone betting on it. Everyone *knew* who was going to win.

When the battle started, David grabbed a rock, pulled back his slingshot, and fired, lodging the rock deep in the skull of the giant warrior, sending him to an early grave.

Everyone may have "known" with equal confidence who was going to win, but only one was right... David.

NEVER STOP BELIEVING IN HOPE BECAUSE MIRACLES HAPPEN EVERY DAY

In 2014, I joined a spin class. Little did I know at the time, but most people in that room were Ironmen. Some were training for their first Ironman, but others had completed at least one Ironman, including the leader, who was an eight-time Ironman! I was in a different league. Or was I? It didn't take more than a few classes for the group to start to encourage me to join them and consider Ironman.

I had to laugh. Me? An Ironman? Seriously? If you are not familiar, Ironman is a race that entails a 2.4-mile swim, followed by a 112-mile bike, which is then followed by a full 26.2-mile marathon run. This is a single race—it's not a multi-day event. My answer was an immediate "No way!" Aside from the stationary bikes in class, I hadn't ridden a bike since I was a kid. I didn't know how to swim, at all. And while I had done distance running in the past, I also sustained a severe running injury five years prior. That injury nearly severed my calf and left my doctors and surgeons in violent agreement—I will never run again. I'm not sure they ever read Matthew 19:26, which says, *"With man this is impossible, but with God all things are possible."*

Coach assured me that he could teach me to swim. But could he teach me to run again, even though the doctors and surgeons had already declared it impossible? I didn't know. All I knew was that Ironman was my Goliath, and I felt like David, the under-equipped, under-prepared, under-talented warrior.

Most people would say, "Let me think about it." I said, "Let me pray on it." As I did, two things happened. First, I came into contact with someone in our church that runs a program for aspiring marathoners, and this team uses the marathon as a way to raise money to build wells in Kenya. The team is called Hope Water Project, and I was told that if I did an Ironman, I could do it as part of the Hope Water Project. Now I had a purpose! I also read a devotional that talked about a Latin phrase, *Deo volente*.

Deo meaning God. *Volente* meaning volition, or will. The idea behind *Deo volente* is that if it's God's will, it cannot be stopped. Good enough for me... I ended up naming my bike *Deo Volente* and eventually made this my motto in life. Needless to say, I was in! It was September 2014, and my targeted Ironman race was September 2015. I had one year to train from zero to full Ironman. Mission impossible? To many, yes. With God on my side, no. *Deo volente.*

As training began, I learned to swim. I also learned to run, and thankfully, I did so without reinjuring myself. Well, for a while...

While my calf remained healthy, I did sustain several knee injuries throughout the season. The worst was a triad of three related knee issues that began in early July, about 11 weeks before my late-September Ironman. It's normal for a marathon runner to "taper" in the 2-4 weeks prior to the actual marathon, as a way to let the legs recover and get energized for the big day. There's no program in the world that supports an 11-week taper. With a knee injury that left me unable to run, I was in trouble. In fact, I tried to run 20 miles just three weeks before the race. I failed. Miserably. Collapsed multiple times in pain, limped many miles, and had to get picked up by car, well short of my goal. Here's the interesting thing... That's about the time I reread the story of David and Goliath. When I reread the story, I realized that David "knew" he would win the battle because his faith carried him. He truly believed beyond any shadow of a doubt that God would lead him to victory. This became my approach, *Deo volente.*

When teammates, friends, and others asked how I was going to get through the run, I simply said, "God will carry me. He always takes care of his people." Much like David and Goliath, we were all equally confident in the outcome, but they were very different outcomes. Clearly they didn't understand who's in charge. Our God provides healing, strength, and wisdom. Clearly they didn't understand that our God is the God of the impossible. They expected me to fail. I boldly declared victory, even when I had no idea if or how my knee would hold up.

Come race day, I prayed, and I believed. During the run, I kept repeating to myself Philippians 4:13, "*I can do all things through Christ who gives me strength."* And as my friends tracked me online, they were in amazement that my time was strong, steady, and never failed. Later they said they had bets on when my knee would give and I'd crash. Not a chance. Those weren't my knees running the race—it was God's race using my body. The crash never happened. I felt no pain whatsoever. None. None. And just saying, but I prayed on it, a ton. Maybe physical therapy was starting to help, and maybe the Motrin was making a difference, unlike my other runs, but that just doesn't add up for me. I absolutely, positively believe there was divine intervention that carried me.

I completed Ironman in just over 11 1/2 hours. In the last mile, the fans lining the side of the road stood and cheered me on. Humbling. As I crossed the finish line, the photographer snapped a picture of me with my arms raised and looking to the sky. If they took a close-up, they would have also seen the tears on my cheeks. And if they added audio, they would have heard my trembling words, as I was all choked up, saying, "Thank you Jesus."

As a side note, that was my first pain-free run in 11 weeks. Three weeks later I ran in the Detroit Marathon, and the pain had returned. And that was without having to bike 112 miles before running my marathon! I still, to this day, cannot explain how I experienced no pain in my Ironman experience, without claiming divine intervention.

"Don't wait for a miracle... Be a miracle!"
~Svetlana Shchedrina

Maybe you believe in God, and maybe you don't. That's not the point. 1980 Miracle on Ice—maybe it was a miracle, and maybe it was just an incredible upset. The near death experience described in Chapter 2—maybe it was a miracle, and maybe it was just an unexplainable, physically impossible event. My Ironman journey, including the lack of race-day injury—maybe it was a miracle, and maybe it was just an unexplainable, miraculous overnight recovery. How you explain the impossible is up to you. But there's no denying that this world is filled with the impossible, each and every day. Believe, embrace, and enjoy.

My Challenge to You

Take just five minutes and think about the following. If you'd like to capture your thoughts on paper, you can do this in Appendix B—Challenge Journal. Or just use your own notebook, or perhaps do it electronically. Regardless of how you do it, just do it.

» Think about all those one-in-a-million aspects of your life.
» Think about the perfect homeostatic balance in your body that keeps your heart beating in the perfect range to support life, that keeps your lungs breathing in the perfect range to support life, the internal changes that keep your pH and chemistry in the perfect range to support life.
» Think about the miracle of birth.
» Think about how the universe is perfectly architected to support life, and how all of the celestial bodies are in perfect alignment such that they rotate around each other and continue to provide an environment suitable for life.
» Think about every strange coincidence you've had or maybe are having now.
» Think about how every decision you've ever made has shaped your destiny.

Now ask yourself again... do you believe in miracles?

CHAPTER 4

BELIEVE IN YOURSELF

"Whether you think you can, or you think you can't—
you're right"

~Henry Ford

THERE ARE TWO MINUTES LEFT in the game, and your favorite football team is up 13–0. The other team hasn't been able to score for 58 minutes, and if nothing changes, they probably won't score again for the remaining two. Victory seems inevitable. But then something happens... your team goes into a "prevent defense." Although this is supposed to prevent them from losing, somehow you get nervous. And notice the subtle twist... for the first 58 minutes they were playing to win; now, for the last two minutes, they are playing not to lose. Naturally, the fact that their minds are focused on not losing, they're thinking about things that really haven't crossed their minds for 58 minutes—like losing. And inevitably, their bodies follow their minds to defeat.

The body always moves in the brain's dominant direction. Have you ever been told to not think of something?

Naturally, you thought of it and couldn't stop thinking about it. Imagine right now if I told you to deliberately not picture anything that's the color blue. Nothing. No blue! If you're like most people, you immediately pictured something blue.

We've all seen the crime dramas on TV in which one lawyer asks the question, "*So, Mr. Smith, do you normally beat your wife?*" Even though the question is ultimately retracted, the damage is done. The lawyer has planted a seed in the minds of the jurors that Mr. Smith beats his wife.

Consider the Bible story of Adam and Eve. They lived in paradise—the most beautiful place, no pain, no worries, no problems. They were just told they couldn't eat from one tree. No big deal. Chances are, they really didn't even want to eat from that tree. Until... the serpent came along and tempted them with lies of power. Now that the seed was planted in their minds, they couldn't stop thinking about it. Eventually, their character couldn't withstand the temptation, and they succumbed. (Genesis 2)

Do you get the picture? Your mind is much more powerful than most people ever imagine! Your thoughts drive your actions, and most of this is done in your subconscious. That's why programming your mind and body for success is so critical in life.

THE BODY ALWAYS MOVES IN THE BRAIN'S DOMINANT DIRECTION

Earlier, I shared my story of Ironman in the context of being a miracle. And trust me, if you had seen me when the journey began, it was truly a miracle. This time, let's look at it from a slightly different perspective.

When I first started, the spin instructor, who is also a certified USA Triathlon Ironman coach, looked me in the eye and said, "*You have what it takes. I want you on my team.*" I laughed because I couldn't swim at all and my previous calf injury resulted in the doctors all telling me I'd never run again. I didn't believe in myself. Yet he persevered with those words, "*I believe in you.*" I still didn't believe, and to prove my point I jumped in the pool in front of him and began swimming as hard as I could. After 16 meters,

I clung to the lane barrier for dear life, unable to complete a single length of the pool. Yet he persevered, *"You can do this. Trust me. I still believe in you."* He did the same thing with running. We committed to focus and act on his belief, and I'm not sure when, but shortly thereafter I said to myself, "This guy saw something I never imagined, but I think he may be right."

As mentioned earlier, I prayed on this and decided to give it a shot. But still, I doubted myself. I tried every excuse to not start training. I kept reminding my coach of the fact that I couldn't swim a length of the pool. I also continually reminded him that I had doctors who had told me I'd never run again. Coach persisted, *"You got this. I believe in you."* Funny how those words can shape a destiny.

THE WORDS "I BELIEVE IN YOU" CAN SHAPE A DESTINY

Little by little, Coach John's persistence won me over. In body, not in spirit. I still didn't believe in me. But as we started swimming, as we started cycling more, and as we started running, I started to believe in me. Once I learned to swim a lap, and then two, and then more, I started to believe. Once I started running a few miles without pain, I started to believe. Once the team formed and I was surrounded by high-caliber athletes with Ironman attitudes, I began to truly believe in me. And once I began truly believing in me, the result was a foregone conclusion.

BELIEVE IN YOURSELF, AND PROGRAM YOUR MIND AND BODY FOR SUCCESS

When I played basketball in my early high school days, I was the last man picked for the team. One time I was talking with the coach, and he was more honest with me than I had hoped. But his honesty changed my paradigm and taught me a valuable lesson. He said, *"VanEpps, I didn't pick you for this team because you've got more talent than the next guy. You don't. But what you lack in talent, you make up for in attitude and heart."* In retrospect, he was right. I was slow, couldn't jump well, was at best an okay shooter, and had below-average ball-handling skills. But I had an un-deniable work ethic. I worked harder than anyone, tried harder than anyone, and always pushed myself.

Later in high school I had a gym teacher who was also the high school football coach. I had never played football in my life, but as a gym teacher he was able to work with me and see me participate in sports. As mentioned above, I wasn't the most athletic person in the class. But for some reason, he looked me in the eye and said, "*VanEpps, you got what it takes. I believe in you. I want you on my team, and I will get you a college scholarship.*" Not sure why, but for some reason I believed him. That belief turned into focus and action. I hit the weights, I ate right, I started running, I was doing double sessions in the blazing sun that summer while my friends were all partying at the beach. That summer I worked harder than I ever imagined possible, and I got myself into the best shape of my life. And somewhere along the way, my mindset changed. I started believing IN myself. When it came time for training camp, I was ready. With a few more boosts from the coach, and with the help of some great mentors, I started to learn the intricacies of the game. I was set up for a very fun and exciting season. Thanks to knee surgery, my football story didn't go much further.

However, one of my college application essays was about this story and my transformation. It was the story of how I went from having no experience and no belief in myself to creating goals, creating supporting action plans, and executing diligently against those plans. It had everything to do with learning to believe in myself and seeing my hard work pay off. Because of this essay, I earned a college scholarship. And while I didn't end up playing football in college, this moment led to my decision of college, which led to my career path, which led to the people I'd meet, which ultimately led to my destiny. See the connection? Those four words, "I BELIEVE IN YOU," shaped my destiny.

Isn't it funny? The coach promised me he'd get me a college scholarship. He did. Not for my quality of play, but for the life lessons acquired in the process. The body always moves in the dominant direction of the brain. Life's not just about the destination—it's about the journey.

EMPOWERING. POWERFUL. ACTION-ORIENTED. LIFE-CHANGING...

Did you ever have a parent say, *"You can do it. I believe in you"*? What about a teacher who maybe changed your life or your kids' lives? What about a mentor, coach, leader, manager, friend who maybe changed your career? What about a spouse who maybe changed your entire life? We all have.

We've been taught since an early age the power of belief. How many of you remember the story of the little engine that could? The little engine THOUGHT it could, but it wasn't until it believed in itself and said, "I know I can" that it was able to clear the summit.

THE POWER OF SELF-BELIEF CAN CHANGE THE WORLD AND SHAPE YOUR DESTINY

What does it mean to "believe in yourself"? My simple answer is that you have self-confidence (not arrogance) that drives positive action. For example, I had a friend at college who allegedly believed in himself. He was always confident that he would ace every test. Unfortunately, that didn't drive action, and his lack of action (homework, studying) caused him to fail out of school. I compare that to one of my daughters, Tori, who is unbelievably smart (no, I'm not biased... much). Tori has confidence, but that confidence says to her, "You can do this. If you work hard at this, results will naturally follow." Tori spent years in competitive dance, where she had to diligently manage her time, and more importantly she had to deliver an exceptional performance over and over. She and her team won many top awards at the national level. This didn't happen by luck. Vince Lombardi said, *"Luck is what happens when preparation meets opportunity."* Tori didn't rely on luck, and she still doesn't. She knows that preparation is key. And preparation is hard work. To this day, she studies hard and works hard, and that positive action has yielded her exceptional results as a student, an athlete, and an extraordinary young woman.

To me, the difference is what I call "believing IN versus just believing." Believing is nothing more than hope. I believe that my favorite sports team, the Detroit Red Wings, will win every hockey game they play, but that doesn't mean anything. It simply means I hope they will win. That belief doesn't drive any action. That belief doesn't program my mind and body for success. However, when it comes to my own athletics, I've learned to believe IN myself. That's not to say I'm arrogant. I'm not. But I know that because I've been born of the seeds of greatness and designed for accomplishment, I can set a goal, create an action plan to achieve that goal, and execute against that plan. And I believe IN myself, such that if I execute against that plan, the resulting success is a foregone conclusion.

BELIEVING IN SOMEONE OR SOMETHING DRIVES THOUGHT, FOCUS, AND ACTION, WHICH PROGRAMS YOUR MIND AND BODY FOR SUCCESS

The biggest challenge is that too often we only believe—we don't believe IN. We don't believe IN ourselves. We don't believe IN ourselves to the point of driving action. Too often we fail to hear others when they say they believe IN us. We hear the words, but we fail to listen. We fail to understand why they believe in us, what they see in us that makes them believe, and allow ourselves to then accept and transfer their belief in us into our own belief in us.

Too often we also miss the opportunities to tell other people that we believe in them. Life is filled with opportunities. You know, those moments that we too often miss and end up kicking ourselves. Those moments alone with our spouse. Those magic times with our kids. Please, please, please don't miss those opportunities. YOU. Yes, YOU. You can change the world by changing lives one at a time—all through the words "I believe in you."

Here's a special callout to leaders. And by leaders, I mean everyone who is in a position to lead, influence, inspire, motivate, guide, mentor, or help others. I think that means you!!! For those people in your dominion—your spouse, your children, your family, your friends, your volunteer groups, your office, your neighbors, etc.—you've been given a very important, life-changing mission. It is not only recommended, but it's incumbent on you to instill value and confidence upon those in your dominion. Speak words of truth. Speak words of hope. Speak words of belief. Change hearts, change minds, and change lives.

SO LET ME ASK YOU, HONESTLY:

- » Do you believe that you were born of the seeds of greatness?
- » Do you believe that you were architected with perfection and designed for accomplishment?
- » Do you believe that you were created for a purpose, something much bigger than yourself?
- » Do you believe that you have what it takes to succeed?
- » Do you believe that it's not just your ability but your destiny to change the world, one life at a time?

YOU must believe IN you. I believe in you. I believe in you because you picked up this book and have at least read it this far. It tells me that you're willing to believe in yourself—you have the confidence and are taking action to make a difference. Something in you believes that you can be more. You get it when I tell you that you were born of the seeds of greatness, you were carefully architected with perfection and designed for accomplishment. You were built to fulfill destinies far greater than yourself, far greater than your self-perceived limits, and far greater than most humans ever imagine possible. You were designed to take chances, to live life, to take risks, and to make a difference. But YOU must believe IN you.

Life's short, and there are a million excuses waiting for you. You can always take the easy way out, you can always rationalize why you didn't give it 100%, and there are plenty of people who will listen and commiserate. But that's not what we were called to do. We were designed for accomplishment. We were put on this planet to fulfill destinies far greater than ourselves. Make the most of it. Take a chance. Step out of your comfort zone. Believe in yourself. And enjoy the journey.

My Challenge to You

Take just five minutes and think about the following. If you'd like to write down your answers, you can do this in Appendix B—Challenge Journal. Or just use your own notebook, or perhaps do it electronically. Regardless of how you do it, just do it.

» Think about opportunities where you could believe in yourself—at work, as a parent, as a spouse, in your community, in your hobbies, financially, spiritually. Why don't you? What's holding you back?
» Are there places in life where someone has expressed their belief in you, but you've rejected their input? Why? Do you think maybe they see potential in you that you don't?
» Are there opportunities to pay it forward? Where might you believe in others? Have you told them? Have you encouraged them? Have you let them know that they have what it takes?

Seek out those moments, those opportunities, those chances to express your belief in others. Mindfully listen when people say to you, *"You can do it."* And believe!

CHAPTER 5

NO LIMITS!

"Goals too often prescribe performance limits!"
~Dr. Fred Hatfield

FOR HUNDREDS OF YEARS BEFORE 1954, running a mile in under four minutes was deemed physically impossible. It didn't just seem impossible; it was scientifically determined that humans were incapable of doing so. Then Roger Bannister did it on May 6, 1954 with a time of 3:59. Within a year, someone else ran a four-minute mile. Now, it's almost routine.

The worst four letter word in the English language is "can't." I can't. No two words in history have imposed more false limitations than the words "I can't." The brain always moves in the direction of one's dominant thoughts. Yet our lives are filled with those words. Trust me, I know. I can't control my diet. I can't lose weight. I can't reduce my blood pressure. The words "I can't" aren't just words—they're a crystal clear set of instructions for your brain, which in turn negatively programs your body for failure. They tell you that something is impossible, and your subconscious goes into autopilot. So think about that when you tell your kids they can't do something—you aren't just saying they cannot do it right now, you're systematically programming their brains that it's not possible for them to do something!

Six years ago, I found myself facing several "I can't" situations. I was overweight by 50 pounds, and I was stuck there. I tried to change my diet, I tried to change my exercise, but I just couldn't lose weight. Since my early 20s, I had been a powerlifter, and gaining weight as I was packing on muscle was no big deal. Whenever I stepped on the scale, I convinced myself that my above-average weight was solely due to muscle. Ha, how many of us have tricked ourselves into believing THAT myth? I then handcuffed myself by saying, "I can't." At the same time, my triglycerides (fat levels in the blood) were the third highest my doctor had ever seen, my blood pressure had been dangerously high since I was 15 years old, my cholesterol was dangerously high, and my sugar was borderline diabetic. To quote my doctor, *"Dave, you are obese, and you're in the high-risk category for heart disease and stroke."* Wake up call…

THE ONLY LIMITS ARE THE SELF-IMPOSED LIMITS YOU CREATE

Too often we limit ourselves by negative programming. There's an old African proverb that says, *"If there is no enemy within, the enemy outside can do us no harm."* We've all had those moments of doubt. You're not good enough. You don't have what it takes. You can't do it. You won't succeed. You're a failure. The truth is, we don't know our own limitations, and too often we allow others, or worse yet ourselves, to impose artificial limitations.

Rewind 20 years, when I was the weightlifter in the corporate fitness center. In this fitness center, there were a bunch of guys who would run at lunch. As they were running, I was hitting the weights. We would banter back and forth about who the greater athletes were, and quite honestly there never was and never will be an answer. Each group had their own thing, and it worked for us. One of the runners, Carl, kept asking me to run with the group. Carl was 20 years older than me, and he was about the nicest guy on the planet. I humbly declined and told Carl that I couldn't even run from the fitness center to the door. And then I'd get him back by challenging him to a squat contest.

A year later, I'd sustained a series of shoulder injuries that dramatically limited my ability to lift. I couldn't do most upper body exercises, and even squats and deadlifts were out of the picture due to my injury. Along came Carl. He didn't rub it in my face. He simply asked, *"Hey, Dave, would you like to learn to run? I could make a marathoner out of you yet."* I laughed at him (do you see a trend here?). Me, a marathoner? Not a chance. I don't run; I lumber like an elephant. Running a mile would be an accomplishment. Running 26.2 miles was out of the realm of possibility. Carl simply said, *"Okay, want to run a mile?"*

We ran one mile, which turned into five. I'm not sure how, but we got talking, and he ran slowly just to engage me in the sport. Carl turned out to be a great mentor. He didn't mention the word *marathon* again. We slowly built up our mileage, and we became friends in the process. At one point, our 7-8 mile daily runs turned into a single 10-mile run. I couldn't believe my body was capable of going that far. Not me, not fat Dave, not the weightlifter, not the guy who could squat 507 pounds. Yes, I remember that number because at the time that was exactly 50% of Dr. Fred Hatfield's world record squat of 1,014 pounds. But I was confident in my ability to lift heavy weights; I wasn't confident in my ability to run. But I digress.

After a few 10-mile runs, Carl backed the mileage down until one day we hit our 5-mile turnaround point for the 10-mile course, and instead of turning around, he asked if we could go just a little farther. Turns out we went 1.55 miles farther, which made our entire run 13.1 miles—a half marathon. That day, Carl asked me to commit to running a marathon with him and a few other friends. Needless to say, I did, we did, and the result is a foregone conclusion.

YOU WERE BUILT TO FULFILL DESTINIES FAR GREATER THAN YOURSELF, FAR GREATER THAN YOUR SELF-PERCEIVED LIMITS, AND FAR GREATER THAN MOST HUMANS EVER IMAGINE POSSIBLE

What if Roger Bannister bought into the current thinking in the early 1950s and accepted the "fact" that the human body was incapable of running a four-minute mile? What if he said, *"I can't"*? It's possible that we still might be trying to surpass that barrier.

In fact, I often ask myself, what if I accepted the fact that I had high blood pressure and couldn't change it? What if I accepted the fact that I had high cholesterol and triglycerides and couldn't change them? What if I accepted the fact that I couldn't run a marathon or complete an Ironman? The answer is simple—my destiny would have changed for the worse. I could be dead. I could be on tons of medications. I could still be at high risk for heart disease, stroke, and diabetes. I could still be overweight by 50 pounds. Thankfully, that's not the case.

Here's the simple truth; everyone loves to see a comeback. Everyone loves to see the underdog overcome all odds. Why do you think the *Rocky* movie turned into a series of never-ending movies? It's because everyone loves the theme—overcoming all odds, establishing a legacy, and winning amidst seemingly impossible circumstances.

My destiny is to create a winning legacy for my family for generations to come. I'm happy to report that hard work, perseverance, health, success, and overcoming all odds are part of that legacy. That's what I want for my children and their children. And guess what... that's what I want for you!!! Let's face it, I could have just told all of these stories to my children if I wanted, and trust me, I have. But I want you to enjoy the journey. I want you to define and fulfill your legacy for generations to come.

YOU WERE DESIGNED TO TAKE CHANCES, TO LIVE LIFE, TO TAKE RISKS, AND TO MAKE A DIFFERENCE. LIVE LIFE TO THE FULLEST. CARPE DIEM... AND JUST GO FOR IT. I PROMISE YOU THE JOURNEY OF A LIFETIME THAT YOU WON'T REGRET.

Let's do this!!!

My Challenge to You

I want you to make a 10-minute appointment with your-self. Carve out the time, and hold yourself accountable to it. Turn off your phone. Turn off your laptop. No Facebook, no Twitter, no texting, no Snapchatting. This needs to be solitary time with just you and your thoughts. Have nothing but a pen and paper. It's time to brainstorm. For your convenience, you can do this in Appendix B—Challenge Journal if you'd like. Or just use your own notebook, or perhaps do it electronically. Regardless of how you do it, just do it.

I want you to start listing every limitation that exists in your life. For example, I'm not a morning person. I can't wake up. I can't control my portions. I can't stop eating junk. I can't lose weight. I can't stop smoking. I can't control my drinking. I can't control my temper. I can't run under a 12-minute mile. I can't bench more than 125 pounds. I can't stop watching Internet porn. I can't stay patient when I'm in traffic. I can't earn more than $50,000 a year. I can't meet the right person. You get the picture—list out where you sometimes or often find your-self saying, "I can't."

Get it all out. Get it on paper. Let's start to wrap our arms around our artificial, self-imposed boundaries. And then let's start figuring out how to crush those falsehoods!

Here we go...

CHAPTER 6

EMBRACE CRISIS

"There are no bad experiences, there are only experiences"

~R. Moore

M Y FRIEND BOB COINED THE above phrase and uses it all the time. Bob is larger than life. He performs at level 10 every day. He redefines the term "high energy." People just love being around this guy—positive, brings out the best in you, magnetic personality, and amazingly powerful people skills. Bob has a real estate venture on the side, which he's appropriately named "WCB Enterprises." WCB is one of his many catch phrases, and it stands for What Could be Better. That's how Bob lives each and every day—believing that the good old days are here and now, and the best is not only yet to come but it's already here, right in front of our faces. The first time Bob used "*There are no bad experiences, there are only experiences*" with me, I laughed. I said, "If you go home today and get in a wreck and lose your leg, isn't THAT a bad experience?" Without missing a beat, he said, "*Only if you let it be.*"

LIFE HAPPENS... IT'S HOW YOU DEAL WITH IT THAT SETS YOU APART

In my late teens and early twenties, I volunteered in a fire department, and I pulled the occasional night shift. One evening, our captain led us in some training drills. As he prepared to leave, one of my fellow firefighters jokingly said, "*See you at the big one.*" Our captain laughed, as we were a small department and rarely had "the big one." The three of us bantered back and forth for a few minutes about showing up at "the big one." In fact, at one point, the comment was made, "*Come on, John, if the big one involved your house, you would show up, right?*" About two hours later, I woke out of a sound sleep to the fire whistle. As I jumped out of bed, I was shocked to hear what the dispatcher said next. "*We have a report of a structure fire, multiple calls confirming flames shooting at least 60 feet.*" I had to pinch myself. There was no way our little department could be having "the big one," especially after the conversation that had just transpired. Then the dispatcher gave the address, and I had to pinch myself again. The address was that of our captain's family business. Not only were we bantering about the big one, at his house no less, but it turned out to be happening, for real, two hours after we were bantering about it.

I'm not sure what happened to me next, but I went into a mini state of shock. I thought that maybe this was a bad dream. There was no way this could be happening for real—too freaky of a coincidence! As the dispatcher's voice came over the radio a second time, I knew it was for real. We hopped on the truck, headed out of the firehouse, and as we turned the corner, our worst fears were confirmed—it was "the big one." The impossible was happening.

We took care of the fire, but then we had to face our captain. I'm not sure I've ever been so scared in my life, as I was praying that I would die before he killed me. After all, this WAS a bad experience. Our captain had too much class to kill us, and in fact, he put one arm around each of us and said, "*Gentlemen, I know you had nothing to do with this, and I understand that this is all just a really weird coincidence. It's okay.*" Phew, he didn't kill us. I still remain thankful that the investigators identified the cause of the fire as being an electrical wiring issue. Then he turned lemons into lemonade. He reminded us that no lives were lost, which is top priority. He reminded us that the adjacent structures were protected, which is second priority. He reminded us that they had insurance and that it would be rebuilt. He even joked at one point about it being free advertising for the business and that maybe they would be better off in the long run. Then he used it as a teaching opportunity for some of us junior firefighters. By any stretch of the imagination, our captain could have declared this a bad experience. Instead, he turned it into a positive.

EXPERIENCE IS WHAT YOU GET WHEN YOU DON'T GET WHAT YOU WANT

There's another well-known story about Thomas Giannettino. Giannettino, a New York State trooper, was working one night when he was assaulted and sustained a severe shoulder injury. With dramatically reduced arm mobility, Thomas had to undergo multiple surgeries and extensive therapy. Ultimately, he wasn't able to continue his career as a state trooper. He began to suffer from depression and PTSD. This was a bad experience... or was it?

Eventually Giannettino's situation did a 180-degree turnaround. He began to participate in the sport of paratriathlon—triathlon for paraplegics. With minimal arm mobility, he had to learn to swim with one arm. However, the more he trained, the better he got. Eventually, he got so good that he was invited to wear the red, white, and blue as he represented Team USA. The story continues. In one interview, he said, "*Some of us are fortunate to have found a spark and a small moment of hope—the hope to push through a devastating time in our lives and to keep fighting to try to find a purpose.*" Did you hear those words—spark, hope, purpose? Those are the words of a winner. He's since become not only a nationally recognized elite para-athlete, but he's also become a sign of hope and inspiration for many who are lost and off course. For more details or to support Giannettino's cause, check out his GoFundMe page at www.gofundme.com/lfswm8.

"A ship in port is safe, but that's not what ships are built for"

~Grace Hopper

Another similar story has to do with an Olympic hero, Cliff Meidl. Meidl was working on a construction site at age 20. In the course of his work, he was severely electrocuted—to the point of going into cardiac arrest. Against all odds, paramedics revived him. After countless surgical procedures and plenty of time in rehabilitation, Meidl's legs still lacked the strength to walk. You might call this a bad experience; Meidl made something of it.

A lifetime athlete, he began to pursue sports that were less dependent on leg strength. He started canoeing and eventually started canoe and kayak racing. Turns out, he was pretty darn good at it, and he continued to rapidly improve. After several years, Meidl made it to the Olympics, representing Team USA as an Olympic rower. For his full story, check out www.cliffmeidl.com.

THERE ARE NO BAD EXPERIENCES, THERE ARE ONLY EXPERIENCES

I was climbing the corporate ladder—great, secure, stable, well-paying job. I was steadily being promoted, and it seemed like I was on a perfect trajectory in my career. And then... I had an opportunity to go work for a start-up company in the dot-com space. I wasn't sure why I would ever leave this career, except that it was only a well-paying job with promise of the standard 2-3% raise every year. By no stretch was it a great-paying job. The dot-com world offered great pay, a great promotion, much more responsibility, challenge, adventure, growth, opportunity, stock options... Oh yeah, it also offered risk. I took it.

I absolutely loved this job! The seven of us in the company truly owned it. We were accountable for everything.

It was a small team, so we all just rolled up our sleeves and got the work done. It was fun, cool, challenging... And then... One Friday our CEO held a team meeting, in which he thanked us for our hard work, and then he informed us that we had effectively volunteered the prior week. He couldn't make payroll. We folded that day.

CRISIS IS OPPORTUNITY

Crisis wasn't opportunity in my mind. Quite frankly, it was the worst thing that had ever happened... at the time. I had two young kids, a new house with a mortgage that was already pushing the limits, and now I was collecting unemployment. Not good!

It wasn't more than a few weeks when I started getting phone calls, including one call from someone who was offering me a job at an even higher level with even higher pay. How could this be? I quickly realized that I was no longer in the open job market at my previous job title and pay—I was now starting from where I was at the start-up company. In a matter of six months, I took two jumps in title and almost doubled my pay. I could have spent my entire life at the original company and never doubled my pay. Never, ever, ever. Certainly not in six months.

Several years later, because of my experience in that job, I received a phone call asking me if I'd be interested in a new opportunity at another company—another big bump in pay and responsibility. Funny how a seemingly tragic situation turned out to be a huge blessing in disguise.

"A CRISIS IS AN OPPORTUNITY RIDING THE DANGEROUS WIND" ~CHINESE PROVERB

If any of you are avid snorkelers or scuba divers, you've undoubtedly swum amidst coral. In protected areas, such as bays or lagoons, the coral is notably lackluster. However, when the coral is in the danger of the tides, predators, and the elements, its colors are the most vivid. Without challenge, without purpose, without stress, the coral in the "easy" environment simply exists. However, the coral that is constantly facing adversity thrives and flourishes.

How many times have you heard about someone who retires and then dies shortly thereafter? Or professional athletes who are still young, yet after retirement they have a major heart attack. Why? We're a lot like coral. In order to thrive and flourish, we need challenge, we need adversity, and we need to be constantly growing and improving ourselves.

"Where there is no vision, the people perish"
~Proverbs 29:18

In Chapter 3, I shared the story of my triad of knee injuries that popped up 11 weeks before my Ironman. This was a crisis. I knew it would be physically impossible for me to successfully finish the race. So was there an opportunity? I didn't see it. Nevertheless, there was. It was an opportunity to spend more time on the bike and radically improve my cycling. It was an opportunity to get more time in both the lake and pool and not only improve my swimming but also learn how to better handle the adversity of open water swimming. It was an opportunity for me to prepare my race strategy and nutrition strategy to perfection, knowing that I would need everything else to be flawless in order to have a chance. It worked.

This year I've had a torn rotator cuff (shoulder), which has severely impacted my training. Again, it was a crisis when it started, but I also realized it would be an opportunity. I just didn't see how. I would never be able to swim 2.4 miles with a torn rotator cuff. With the help of our team's swim coach, I've learned how to effectively do a multitude of kicks and different strokes. Now, despite the fact that my surgeon won't let me start swimming freestyle again this season, I remain confident that this crisis gave me the opportunity to be stronger and better than ever.

WHAT DOESN'T KILL ME ONLY MAKES ME STRONGER

Most of us have heard the story of Bethany Hamilton, the Soul Surfer. Bethany was a competitive surfer with dreams of becoming a professional, when at age 13, a shark attacked her. The shark bit off her left arm, which seemingly would have shattered her hopes and dreams. By most standards, this was a crisis.

Not for Bethany. She turned this crisis into an opportunity. She was surfing within a month of the attack. Just one year after the attack, she leveraged this opportunity to write her autobiography entitled *Soul Surfer: A True Story of Faith, Family, and Fighting to Get Back on the Board.* She now had a global audience and a perfect soapbox on which to tell her story! She also fulfilled her dream of becoming a professional surfer.

LIVE OUTSIDE YOUR COMFORT ZONE. TAKE RISKS. LIVE LIFE

Every crisis in my life has proven to have an opportunity on the other end. They've all played a role in who I am, what I stand for, and who I will become. Even when I couldn't see the opportunity, it was there. Moreover, I assure you no matter what crisis you're going through in life, there's an opportunity. It's this resilience and perseverance that build character.

The easy way out will always be there. You can quit. You can fail. You can blame your circumstances. Those make great stories for your local bartender. But they don't make great stories for your audience. They don't make great stories for your family and future generations. They want to hear how you struggled, how you overcame adversity, how you never quit, how you defied all odds, how you changed the paradigm, and how you ultimately made a difference in their future. The choice is yours.

My Challenge to You

Just take five minutes and think about this. For your convenience, you can do this in Appendix B—Challenge Journal if you'd like. Or just use your own notebook, or perhaps do it electronically. For this exercise, maybe you don't want to write anything down, just think. Regardless of how you do it, just do it.

Undoubtedly, you have many bad experiences in your life, many of which are going on right now. We're human. We're all imperfect. We like to think everyone else's lives are perfect behind the scenes, but I promise you we are no different and we ALL have experiences we struggle with. Maybe you struggle with alcohol, smoking, gambling, pornography, a challenging marriage, a difficult teenager, a sick child, aging parents, strained family relationships, etc. I challenge you to think about these experiences in this context: "There are no bad experiences, there are only experiences." I challenge you to ask yourself:

- » What are you being taught?
- » What part of your character is being molded?
- » How is this making you stronger?
- » How is this making you more resilient?
- » How is this teaching you to persevere through adversity?
- » How can you use this experience to help yourself and others?
- » How can you use this to change the world and shape a destiny?

SECTION 3

CHANGE YOUR THINKING

CHAPTER 7

WE ALL NEED HELP

"If I have seen further it is by standing on the shoulders of giants"

~Bernard of Chartres

IT WAS A CONFIRMED STABBING. The police had responded to a domestic dispute, and upon arrival they quickly learned that the dispute had gone south. There was blood everywhere, as the angry girlfriend had pulled out the steak knife and planted it squarely in her boyfriend's (maybe ex-boyfriend at that point) chest. Dispatch called my unit to respond. It was a very small alley off a very small road, and we didn't go into this neighborhood often. We pulled out our street index to see exactly where we were going, and guess what page was missing? Yep, the page with the street we needed. This was before the days of smartphones, OnStar, GPS, and cool navigation apps like Waze. We had an old-fashioned street index, and it wasn't going to help. We quickly got lost, our response time was getting longer and longer, and the patient's condition was getting worse and worse. My partner and I were afraid to ask dispatch for instructions. Not only would it be obvious that we were lost, but we also ran the risk of this call being reassigned to another ambulance. Neither would be a good outcome. Having no other option, we finally swallowed our pride, got directions from dispatch, and the situation turned out as well as it could. I can't say what happened to their relationship, but the boyfriend lived and fully recovered.

Has any guy in the history of mankind ever asked for directions? Likely no, and thanks to modern technology, we never have to anymore! To me, asking for directions is a way of saying I failed. It represents a way of saying I can't do it. It's a way of saying, "Here you go, just take my man card." No guy likes to ask for directions. In fact, few of us ever like to ask for help, at all.

"You can do anything, but not everything"
~David Allen

My undergraduate degree is in computer science, and my graduate degree is in software development and management. Most of my career has been spent in information technology. At heart, I'm a geek, although I gave up my pocket protector in the 1980s. Just kidding—never had one. One of the challenges software engineering has always faced has been the NIH syndrome—Not Invented Here. For decades, software engineers wrote their own code, even when someone else had already written code to perform the exact same function. Maybe it's more fun, maybe it's a little arrogant, but every software engineer believes that he/she can write code that's better than anything else out there.

I remember a Christmas party in the early 1990s in which our organization's vice president proclaimed that we were switching to a new software engineering approach and that this new approach would yield a 10x improvement in productivity. Yeah, right. Maybe when pigs fly...

However, this approach did introduce the idea of reusability to our organization. Reusability is a technical word that makes people sound intelligent, but it's really about standing on the shoulders of giants. If someone already wrote software to perform a given function, don't start from scratch to write it all over—just use it again (reuse)! As a software engineer early in my career, I quickly learned how to stand on the shoulders of giants. In school we had always been taught not to plagiarize, but suddenly this idea of reusability actually encouraged plagiarism! How cool is that?

> *"Don't reinvent the wheel, just realign it"*
> *~Anthony D'Angelo*

I learned to stand on the shoulders of giants in other aspects of my life as well.

Most of my life, I felt that anyone who put their trust and faith in God was weak. I thought that religion was an excuse, a crutch fabricated by little old ladies who couldn't manage life. Until I hit a point where I was feeling overwhelmed. Work projects from hell, health issues, my inability to lose weight, and life in general were getting the best of me. I was at the point where I was pretty sure God didn't want anything to do with me anyway. I'd pretty much broken all of his rules and had skipped church more often than not over the last dozen or so years. Based on my false definition of God and his expectations, I had fallen short beyond the point of recovery.

One day I tried a new church and had my first positive church experience ever. I kept going back for several months until one day I finally realized that we're all broken and messed up. More importantly, I realized that's okay! God knows we're messed up, but He still loves us and longs for a relationship. He is willing to meet us where we are, in our brokenness, and help us. Most importantly, because Jesus died for us, forgiveness is a foregone conclusion.

I recognized my weakness, and literally fell to my knees asking for help. It was humbling. After all, I was a weightlifter, a powerlifter, a strong guy with a great job and great family. If I need help, then I might as well surrender my man card, right? Wrong. It was the best move I ever made. Funny how the greatest moment of strength in my life came when I realized my own weakness, fell to my knees, humbled myself, and asked God and others for help. My spiritual journey began, and every minute of this story has since shaped my destiny.

But he said to me, "My grace is sufficient for you, for my power is made perfect in weakness"
~2 Corinthians 12:9

I have mentioned a few times about the struggles I had with weight, diet, and my blood work. I spent years trying to figure it out. I read books, researched on the Internet, and studied all I could. Unfortunately, nutrition is an area of extreme information overload, and because of all the conflicting information, it can be confusing to say the least. Are carbs good or bad? Is wine good or bad? Is eating fat good or bad? I just couldn't make sense of it, and I was getting nowhere fast.

At the risk of my man card, I realized it was time for help. Again, can you see a pattern here? I hated to ask for directions, I thought spiritual people were weak, and I could never have imagined asking for help with nutrition. Let me tell you, asking for help was another brilliant move! I was connected with the most amazing, talented nutritionists (Nuview Nutrition in Clarkston, MI—they're awesome). They had me fill out a detailed questionnaire, provide them with my latest lab work, and then I underwent my initial evaluation. It didn't take long for them to realize I was in a bad place and rapidly going in the wrong direction. With a master's degree, a good job, and a track record of academic success, I would have liked to think I was intelligent enough to figure this out. Not the case—it was time to stand on the shoulders of giants... again.

Terri and Carly have become my nutritionists. Or as I call them, my nutrition coaches. They worked with me to create an ongoing meal plan, which wasn't a fad diet but rather a paradigm shift in my view of healthy meal planning. They worked with me, using my biometrics as input, and custom-created a meal plan for me. Unlike what I had always read, they really simplified it to the basics.

Eat five meals daily, evenly spaced through the day. Don't eat processed foods. Lots of fruit and vegetables. They also taught me that you can't out-train a bad diet. One would think that Ironman training 15–20 hours a week at high intensity would burn more calories than I could ever consume. Instead, my exercise combined with a bad diet and too few calories was actually putting my body under a dangerous, unhealthy amount of stress, which required dietary adaptations. Then they got to the more difficult stuff, which isn't really that difficult but rather hard to decipher through all the misinformation in the public domain.

Together, we created a program that was healthy, but more importantly, it was sustainable as a lifestyle. This wasn't about dropping some weight and walking away. Like any change worth making, it was about creating a sustainable lifestyle change. And like any change worth making, it involved work. Terri and Carly guided me as I lost over 50 pounds and have managed to keep them off. I've now been at my healthy weight in the 180s for well over a year and counting! The nutrition is also largely responsible for the unbelievable improvements in my blood work. They monitored my progress, adapted my plan as needed, held me accountable to the results, and guided me down the path to success. And we're still going strong!

YOU CAN'T OUT-TRAIN A BAD DIET

Consider my Ironman experience from the perspective of needing help. Could I have done this without a coach? Not likely. Would I have done this without a coach? Not a chance! It's a great concept, but a coach brings so much more to the game. My Ironman coach, John, is independent. Unlike a friend, family member, or spouse, he isn't there to be my friend—he is there to be my coach. We have obviously become friends in that time, but the goal was all about performance. He's there to push me to my limit, and then a tiny bit past. John has repeatedly pushed me outside my comfort zone. He has pushed me to ride and run in the pouring rain and other suboptimal conditions to help build my mental toughness. He's made me do planks for 5, 10, even 20 minutes. Is that necessary for a triathlon? Not at all. Is that necessary to push me out of my comfort zone and to teach my mind to control my body, especially when it's under stress? Absolutely!

Lastly, John is there to hold me accountable. There have been plenty of cold winter mornings when the alarm went off at 4:30, and the thought of jumping in a pool was terrifying. Sure, the pool is indoors, but we generally run a mile to and from the pool—yes, even when we're soaking wet after the swim in the dead of winter. At 4:30, that's a lot of motivation to hit the snooze alarm! But... every time I reach for the snooze, I hear John's voice saying, *"Dave, where were you today? You're an Ironman. Come on, I expect better."* Rise and shine, we've got work to do.

SOMETIMES YOUR GREATEST MOMENT OF STRENGTH IS FALLING ON YOUR KNEES AND ASKING FOR HELP

In 2010, shortly after my doctor had me "call Tony" and start doing P90X, I was connected with a fantastic Team Beachbody Coach, Jeff. Even though Jeff lives nearly 1,000 miles away, we became fast friends. I wasn't sure how he could truly coach me from that far away, but I quickly learned. Jeff and I connected through email, social media, and phone calls. Every day, like clockwork, Jeff asked me to post on social media about my workout. He was holding me accountable. Not once did Jeff ever embarrass me. Not once did Jeff ever make me feel bad if I missed a workout. Quite the opposite. Jeff remains one of the most positive people I've ever met. If I ever missed a workout, Jeff would say, *"Okay, Dave, let's hit it tomorrow. No excuses."* If I ever had a bad workout, Jeff would say, *"It happens to the best of us. Let's keep on going tomorrow."* Always positive, always motivating, always inspiring. Through our relationship, he coached me down the first 18 pounds and to the point of being considerably more fit than I'd been since my teenage years. My level of fitness was key in preparing me for my soon-to-come Ironman journey. Jeff and I still stay close, I'm still part of his Fitness Warriors accountability team, and he remains one of the most positive people on the planet.

Put down your ego. Get over the fact that you're struggling. Everyone's struggling. Everyone wants to improve in at least one part of his or her life. Some just try to fake it and act like everything's perfect. It's not. Don't fake it. Be true to yourself and others. Seek out help. Make the commitment, and just go for it. It's time for the new you.

My Challenge to You

Remember in Chapter 5 when we started creating our list of false, self-limiting beliefs? I'm going to ask you to stand on the shoulders of giants to begin tackling those false beliefs. Yes, you need help. Could you work through the barriers on your own? Quite possibly. But why? Leverage others' success stories to help yourself!

For your convenience, you can do this in Appendix B—Challenge Journal if you'd like. Or just use your own notebook, or perhaps do it electronically. Maybe for this exercise you'd rather just think it through and take action on your own. Regardless of how you do it, just do it. This exercise should take you about 10 minutes.

For each barrier you listed in Chapter 5, start listing out how you're going to seek help. Who can help you?

If you're limited by diet issues—weight, cholesterol, blood pressure, sleep disorders, pain and inflammation, or you just need accountability with your eating—get a coach. See a qualified nutritionist and get an evaluation.

If you're limited by exercise issues—lack of structured workouts, need accountability, lack of progress, stuck on a plateau, questions about different workout programs, unsure where to start—get a coach or a trainer. You can find coaches online; you can find trainers in almost any gym. Go to the Team Beachbody website. They're out there, and they can help. Make sure you check qualifications and references.

If you're limited in your career—job potential, glass ceilings, inability to break into the next level—get a coach. There are plenty of professional and/or executive coaches who specialize in helping people with their careers. If you don't want a coach, get a mentor. There are people in every company who would love nothing more than to pour into the next generation of leaders. I thrive on coaching others, and I see others thrive in helping me. Reach out, ask someone. Don't wait for the introduction of a formal mentoring program—just ask someone who's in a position you'd someday like to be in! Ask someone who's solved the problem that you're trying to solve. Just ask! If you're not comfortable asking, search online for executive coaches.

If you're limited in your finances: excessive debt, inability to create or live on a budget, inability to save for college or retirement, inability to save for a rainy day, or any other financial matters, get help from a financial advisor. I highly recommend a class by Dave Ramsey called *Financial Peace University*. Highly recommend it! I've been through it, and it's made a huge difference in my life. Life transforming. If every high-school/college student took this program, debt would become a thing of the past. Seriously, check it out.

If you're limited in other ways such as addiction, marriage problems, grief, challenging kids, seek help. Alcoholics Anonymous has a great program for recovery—defined steps and accountability partners. There are plenty of great counselors that can help with these issues. I know, churches often have bad reputations, and that's because there are plenty of bad churches. There are also plenty of incredibly amazing churches. My church, Kensington Community Church, offers so many services—grief support, divorce care, recovery from addiction, and much more. They're all done in community with others who have similar struggles. More importantly, they work. Seek out a good, Bible-based church in your area, get some word-of-mouth references, and try it out.

Need help in life? Seek out a life coach. My mentor, Don (www.donstaley.com), is a fantastic life coach. Give it a shot.

Maybe even fall to your knees and ask God for help. Who knows what could happen—it worked for me.

CHAPTER 8

CHANGE THE PARADIGM

*"When we change our paradigms, we make visible
what we couldn't imagine before"*
                                    ~Author Unknown

I ONCE READ AN INTERVIEW in which identical twins, whose parents were alcoholics, were interviewed once they reached adulthood. Their responses will resonate in my head forever. The first twin said, *"Yes, I am an alcoholic. You see, my parents are both alcoholics. I didn't have a choice."* The second twin, when interviewed separately, said, *"No, I don't even drink. You see, my parents are both alcoholics. I didn't have a choice."* Incredible... I didn't have a choice. Same DNA, same environment. Different paradigm, different outcome. Leaders view choices as opportunities. John Wooden once said, *"The choice you make, makes you."* You see, all choices lead you somewhere. The question is, where?

CHANGE YOUR PARADIGM, CHANGE YOUR DESTINY

There's a well-known story about a man named Victor Serebriakoff. When Victor was a teenager, a teacher told him that he was a dunce. Too stupid to continue with school or ever get a job that would require an education. He was strongly encouraged to drop out of school and make a living doing minimum-wage jobs.

For the next 16 years, Victor woke up and looked in the mirror, but a dunce looked back at him. Victor showered the dunce, shaved the dunce, dressed the dunce, and went to the dunce jobs doing dunce work for dunce pay. His paradigm was set—Victor knew his place in life.

Later, in the military, Victor took a test, though he didn't know why. He was convinced it was to prove how much of a dunce he really was. After the test, the proctors called him back. They asked him to take another test. Still convinced it was to prove his low level of intelligence, he agreed. Then it happened again. He ended up taking a third test. Victor was called in to discuss the results, and I'm sure he considered skipping what was inevitably a humiliating, embarrassing conversation. However, when Victor showed up, he was shocked at what he heard.

Victor was informed that he wasn't in fact a dunce. These were IQ tests, and they informed Victor that he was a genius with an IQ of 161. The next day, Victor woke up and looked in the mirror. Only this time, the dunce didn't look back at him. A genius did. Victor showered the genius, shaved the genius, and dressed the genius. Only this time, he didn't go back to the dunce jobs. He went to work as a genius.

Thanks to his new self-image, his new paradigm, Victor became the president of MENSA, which is a society that requires all members to be at or near genius level. He also went on to publish many books, did benevolent work for the Mensa Foundation for Gifted Children, and earned multiple patents in the timber industry.

> *"It's not who you are that holds you back, it's who you think you're not"*
>
> *~Eric Thomas*

I've worked out since I was 16 years old. My father was a huge bodybuilding fan and in his heyday had some killer biceps. Not to mention an impressive squat on his home-made rack. Our basement looked like a hardcore iron gym, and he spent an hour or so down there pumping iron every day. He was an impressive athlete—strong, dedicated, and always focused on improvement. His love for the weights became my love for the weights, and starting at age 16, I became addicted to bodybuilding and powerlifting. He was a true role model in every sense of the word. He also taught me the art of storytelling, and hopefully you're reaping the benefits right now!

Over the years, I started to believe that it's okay to carry some fat if you're powerlifting. In my late 20s and 30s, as I did more powerlifting than bodybuilding, I gained amazing strength. Well, at least it was amazing for me... I didn't realize that my weight gain was mostly fat, not muscle. In fact, when I looked in the mirror, I still saw a bodybuilder looking back at me. I hadn't yet changed my paradigm to realize that a fat guy was looking back at me.

MY QUESTION TO YOU IS, WHEN YOU LOOK IN THE MIRROR, WHO DO YOU SEE?

Then it happened. One day, after my doctor had told me I was obese, I went back and looked in the mirror, and the bodybuilder no longer looked at me. Instead, some fat guy looked at me. Ugh. Amazingly, everywhere I went I saw myself as a fat guy. I was afraid to take off my shirt. I was afraid to change in the locker room. I. Was. Fat.

Sadly, obesity is an American epidemic, and this is a great example of how it happens—one day at a time. Nobody wakes up fat. Nobody eats a pizza and turns fat overnight. It's a deadly process that happens one skipped workout at a time, one bad calorie at a time, one day at a time... Let's face it, every calorie that enters your body counts. Even on your birthday—there's no such thing as a free calorie. Let's not even get into the debate right now. I agree that we need a sufficient supply of calories across a number of meals evenly spaced throughout the day, and when done correctly, calories are good! I get that. But I also get that the occasional cookie counts, the candy bar counts, and all those junk calories we eat without thinking much of it—they count too. Obesity is one of the most expensive diseases to our country, and yet it's the most preventable.

As I mentioned earlier, my doctor made me order P90X, which comes with both an intense exercise program plus a meal-planning guide. When he returned, my doctor then ordered me, "*Start making daily appointments with Tony, NOW!*" His message was loud and clear. Time to overhaul the diet. Time to overhaul the exercise plan. Time to change the paradigm. Welcome to the new you!

Thank God for his honesty... had he tiptoed around the issue, I would have still believed that I was mostly muscle. Had he not directed me on my next step in the action plan, I would not have done a thing differently. It was time to change, and it had to be done right now! What ensued was the next chapter of my life transformation. I began eating according to the P90X meal-planning guide. I began daily exercise using the P90X program. I quickly lost 18 pounds. I quickly started to reshape my body—much less fat, much more lean-muscle mass. I had more strength, more energy, and was looking less and less like the fat guy every day.

> "*The first step to getting anywhere is deciding you're no longer willing to stay where you are*"
> ~J.P. Morgan

I'm currently in my second season of Ironman training. Last year I was the rookie, and amazing things happened when I started believing in myself, as I shared in Chapter 3. This year, I've been able to train with confidence while pouring into the rookies on the team.

I've noticed the transformation in others, which I hadn't completely recognized in myself at the time. Sure, confidence plays into this, and believing in yourself plays into this. No question. But so does paradigm. After the first race of the season, Coach John said to two of our rookies, *"Congratulations, now you are officially a triathlete."* It's just words, right? Wrong! Those words turned Ted and Christina from athletes in training, who would participate in our team training, to complete animals!

It was amazing to watch, but here's the truth of what transpired in the subconscious mind. Both Ted and Christina had seen themselves as trainees. As rookies. Not as triathletes. In fact, when they looked in the mirror, trainees looked back at them. Until after the first race. At that point, when they looked in the mirror, triathletes looked back at them. Their paradigm changed. And I've seen both of them demonstrate a whole new energy level that I didn't think possible, and the daily improvements in both of them is amazing and fun to watch!

IT'S TIME TO BREAK ALL SELF-LIMITING PARADIGMS AND TO LIVE THE LIFE OF EXCELLENCE THAT YOU WERE MEANT TO LIVE!

An affirmation is an effective tool used to address negative self-perceptions. It's a positive statement that is repeated daily for at least 21 days, which is how long researchers believe it takes to change a habit. A key is that the affirmation is stated in the positive and in the present. Avoid negative statements. Instead of saying something like "I'm not fat" try something like "I am lean." Also avoid using future tense. Instead of saying, "I will start eating fewer and better calories" try something like "I eat the right number of calories each day, made up of healthy foods." Positive... Present...

"Sow a thought, reap an action; sow an action, reap a habit; sow a habit, reap a character; sow a character, reap a destiny"
~Stephen Covey

I did this when I was going through the early phases of my journey. Keep in mind, I was fat, I was eating too much junk, I lacked confidence in my ability to change the situation, and I was feeling like I couldn't go to church or ask for God's help because I was a bad enough person that he probably hated me. Here are some affirmations that appeared on my mirror:

» I weigh 190 pounds
» I have 10% body fat
» I am in incredible shape
» I eat five clean meals of 400-500 healthy calories every 3-4 hours
» I am a child of God and am loved immeasurably by Him
» I have what it takes to succeed
» I am born of the seeds of greatness, architected with perfection, and designed for accomplishment

When programming the mind, we need to remember that 95% of our programming occurs in the subconscious brain, and only 5% occurs in the conscious brain. Affirmations are a great way of programming both your conscious and sub-conscious mind. This is a great start, but it's not enough.

"Whatever we plant in our subconscious mind and nourish with repetition and emotion will one day become a reality"
~E. Nightingale

Let's get to work. Start now, wherever you are, what-ever is holding you back, whatever you think of yourself and your situation. It's time to retrain your mind, and if you start with a thought and turn it into an action, you can establish the habits of success. You're worth it! You deserve to live the life you were designed for. So what's stopping you??? Nothing. Let's do this!

My Challenge to You

I want you to make another 20-minute appointment with yourself. Carve out the time, and hold yourself accountable to it. Turn off your phone. Turn off your laptop. No Facebook, no Twitter, no texting, no Snapchatting. This needs to be solitary time with just you and your thoughts.

For your convenience, you can do this in Appendix B—Challenge Journal if you'd like. Or just use your own notebook, or perhaps do it electronically. For this exercise, consider Post-it notes as well. Regardless of how you do it, just do it.

Ask yourself the following questions:

» When I look in the mirror, who is looking back?
» How do I see myself?
» What goals, dreams, and expectations of yourself might be affecting how you see yourself?
» Am I happy with the person who looks back?
» Do I still have some lingering self-limiting beliefs from Chapter 5 that I couldn't tackle by standing on the shoulders of giants?
» Am I hearing other lies that are trying to tell me that I'm not good enough? Or that I don't have what it takes? They're lies—they're wrong. But let's squash them in their tracks, now!

Most people who do this exercise have some positives and some negatives.

Time to start changing the paradigm. For every negative answer, I want you to create an affirmation. Again, an affirmation is a positive statement that you will repeat daily for at least 21 days. I suggest using small Post-it notes and sticking them to your mirror—just remember to take them down before Windexing! You can put them anywhere that's accessible, visible, and will help you establish your affirmations. Remember, the affirmation is stated in the positive and in the present. For the next 21 (or more) days, make a deliberate point to look at these affirmations and say them aloud. At least once a day if not more.

You need to not only program your mind for success, but you need to act upon it to start to drive change. This comes in the next chapter, when we talk about goals. For now, let's just start with identifying our limiting para-digms and creating affirmations to start working on the subconscious.

SET YOUR PRIORITIES

CHAPTER 9

AIM HIGH

Aim high—define yourself, your goals, your destiny

"BUT WHY, SOME SAY, THE moon? Why choose this as our goal? And they may well ask why climb the highest mountain? Why, 35 years ago, fly the Atlantic? ... We choose to go to the moon. We choose to go to the moon in this decade and do the other things, not because they are easy, but because they are hard, because that goal will serve to organize and measure the best of our energies and skills, because that challenge is one that we are willing to accept, one we are unwilling to postpone, and one which we intend to win." ~John F. Kennedy

GO BIG OR GO HOME!

Did you know the most successful 3% of our population has documented, current, relevant goals? The top 3%! So why? What is it that makes that 3% more successful than the remaining 97%? It's simple. Setting goals is a form of programming for your subconscious mind. Highly successful people know where they're going, and they have an action plan to get there. They fully expect to achieve success, and they believe IN themselves.

Yet, what happens every year on December 31st? Everyone makes their New Year's resolutions... to lose weight, to eat healthy, to exercise more, to focus more on their families, to do better at work, etc. On January 2nd, the gyms across the US are filled with well-intentioned people, most of whom paid a one-time fee and monthly dues for the privilege to join the gym. Then by February 1st, those very same gyms are empty again. Back to the same old regulars. Why?

> *"Impotent goals only prescribe performance limits"*
> ~ *Dr. Fred Hatfield*

Think about it; we tend to create lame goals. They're not specific, not measurable, not achievable, not backed by a realistic action plan, not bound by a given date, and quite frankly, boring. A good goal is one that excites you, motivates you, inspires you, and at the same time scares the living crap out of you. A good goal is one that exhilarates you and at the same time exhausts you. A good goal is one that is worth pursuing, regardless of the cost.

DON'T THINK THAT JUST BECAUSE YOU'RE GOOD, YOU DON'T HAVE A WEALTH OF OPPORTUNITY AHEAD!

Early in my career, I read these statistics about the most successful people and goals. I also learned how to set goals. We'll cover that in our challenge below. I decided to give it a try. Here's what I pulled together at the time:

» I will double my current salary in 10 years.
» I will begin contributing 15% of my salary to retirement and be on a plan to retire by age 55.
» I will begin contributing to meaningful charitable causes in three years.

» I will be an executive of a company where I can make an impactful, positive difference to a large team in five years.
» I will bench press 315 in one year.
» I will squat 500 in two years.
» I will someday run a marathon.

As I wrote those goals, I laughed at myself. They were absurd… these were a 4-minute mile. These were like going to the moon. However, the goals workshop I had completed incorporated one key rule: "Don't evaluate!" If it's something you want, write it down. Don't evaluate your ability to get there. Just make note that you want to get there. I did. As ridiculous as it seemed, I did. Especially the marathon goal—I wasn't a runner, hated running, never wanted to run, yet I said it would be a cool bucket list item. That's called programming your subconscious mind!

Three years later, I had made two job changes, and had more than doubled my salary. It didn't take 10 years, it took three. I was also contributing 20% of my salary to retirement and well on my way to retirement by age 55. I was contributing to meaningful causes, and you will read more on that later in this book. I became an executive overseeing and improving a large team within three years. Lastly, I surpassed my fitness goals at the time by benching 350 and squatting 507, both above anything I ever imagined possible. The marathon… that happened just two years after writing down my goals.

THE BODY ALWAYS MOVES IN THE DOMINANT DIRECTION OF THE BRAIN

Let me reiterate… the body always moves in the dominant direction of the brain. Your subconscious represents 95% of your brain. Program your mind and body for success.

SETTING GOALS PROGRAMS YOUR SUBCONSCIOUS MIND

My stepson, Danny, loves hockey. He has a goal—to play in the NHL. No, check that, he wants to win the Stanley Cup and be an NHL all-star. What kid doesn't, right? Is it realistic?

Sure it is... but this goal is programming his conscious mind, subconscious mind, and body for success. The body moves in the dominant direction of the brain. By having the dream of hockey, it programs him to play hockey, skate, practice, work on skills, eat right, stay in shape, study the game, and improve himself. Will he ever become an NHL superstar? Who knows? I hope so—he certainly has amazing potential. But let's ask the more important questions. Is he enjoying life? Is he programming his mind and body for success? Is he becoming a better person, both mentally and physically, because of this goal? The answer is a resounding "Yes!"

What are your goals? How are you programming your mind and body for success?

Hmmm, this sounds pretty easy, right? It is. But it isn't. You need to set good goals. You need to focus. You need to program your subconscious mind. But expect resistance. Every goal worth achieving will be met with some resistance. FUD will try to get the best of you—fear, uncertainty, and doubt. This is the enemy's way of sabotaging your self-improvement efforts. You'll hear words like I heard when I created the goals listed above—you'll laugh at yourself, your goals will seem absurd, and you'll hear words like, "You can't do this," "You're not good enough," "It will never happen." Your mind and body get very comfortable with the status quo, and most of us naturally resist change.

ACCOMPLISHING GOALS REQUIRES YOU TO STEP OUTSIDE YOUR COMFORT ZONE AND BE WILLING TO BE GREATER THAN YOU EVER IMAGINED POSSIBLE

There's a Bible story in which the disciple Peter is in a boat and sees Jesus walking on water. Peter wants to do the same, and Jesus calls him to do so. Peter focuses intently on Jesus, reaches out to Jesus, and starts to walk on water. This is exactly what I'm talking about—focus on your goals and don't be afraid to be wildly successful!!! As Peter steps out of his comfort zone, with complete focus, he successfully takes several steps on the water. Unfortunately, Peter then encounters fear, uncertainty, and doubt. Something inside him reminds him that he's outside his comfort zone. Something inside him says, "You can't do this." At that point, Peter goes under. This story may be 2,000 years old, but it's a picture-perfect depiction of what happens to us whenever we try to step out of our comfort zone. It also tells us what happens when we're focused on our goals versus when we take our eye off the ball. (Matthew 14:25-30)

Yes, it feels uncomfortable at first. But remember, you were born of the seeds of greatness, you were carefully architected with perfection and designed for accomplishment. You were built to fulfill destinies far greater than yourself, far greater than your self-perceived limits, and far greater than most humans ever imagine possible. You were designed to take chances, to live life, to take risks, and to make a difference. So give it a shot. Unless you're living an abundant life already filled with happiness and joy, and unless you have no desire to improve, just go for it.

Aim for the moon. Aim for four minutes. Set your goals, and go get it. Stop at nothing. And when storms come up, I'll leave you with the words of Vince Lombardi, who was amazingly determined and focused on achieving goals. He said, *"We know how rough the road will be, how heavy the load will be, we know about the barricades that wait along the track, but we have set our soul ahead upon a certain goal ahead and nothing left from hell to sky shall ever turn us back."*

YOUR GREATEST COMPETITION ISN'T EXTERNAL, IT'S ALWAYS WITHIN. IT'S YOUR FEAR, UNCERTAINTY, AND DOUBT BATTLING YOU. DON'T LET IT WIN!

Life's not about finding yourself. It's about defining yourself. Let's get out there and define ourselves. New and improved. Phenomenal. Fearless. Relentless. Unafraid to step out of our comfort zone. To take chances. To live life to the fullest—the way you were meant to live.

My Challenge to You

We're going to do a goals workshop. Right now I want you to carve out two 30-minute blocks of time. Just an hour of your time! C'mon, you can do this... I need you to block out this time and follow these instructions:

BLOCK #1: 30 MINUTES

Turn off your phone. Turn off your laptop. No Facebook, no Twitter, no texting, no Snapchatting. This needs to be solitary time with just you and your thoughts. Have nothing but a pen and paper. It's time to brainstorm. Brainstorming means that you keep writing for the entire window. Don't evaluate, just write. For your convenience, you can do this in Appendix B—Challenge Journal if you'd like. Or just use your own notebook, or perhaps do it electronically. Regardless of how you do it, just do it.

First 10 minutes—do nothing but dream. No rules. No evaluation. No boundaries. Pen never stops. Brain never stops. Dream big. Don't limit yourself. Never say never. What's your story? This may be morbid, but write your own obituary—what will people say about you? What's your legacy? What will you be remembered for?

Think about your dream job—your title, your pay, your recognition, how others describe you, the type of environment you work in, your bonus, your perks... What about secondary forms of income—speaking engagements, teaching, training... What about your education—do you want to go back to school, pursue additional degrees, take more courses, personal development opportunities, great books you'd like to read, seminars or conferences you'd like to attend, skills you'd like to obtain.

Think about your family and friends—what type of relationship do you want with them, how do you want to spend your time together, what are things you would like to do, places you'd like to go, ways you'd like to volunteer or do community activities together.

Think about things you'd like to have—what type of house, where would you like to live, what types of possessions would you like. Think about how you spend your time—would you like to volunteer, learn new activities, play sports?

How about financial—when would you like to retire, how much would you like to have when you retire, would you like to get out and stay out of debt, would you like to help others?

How about spiritual—what type of relationship would you like to have with your Creator, how would you like to serve, how would you like to worship?

And think about physical—what is your desired weight, how often would you like to exercise, what types of exercise would you like, do you have any sport-specific goals like running a marathon or 5K, how about bench pressing or squatting a certain weight? What about your eating habits—how many meals a day, how many calories, what types of foods, etc.?

Anything else you can think of that you would like to have in life? Keep writing until the 10 minutes are up.

CONGRATULATIONS, YOU'VE COMPLETED THE FIRST STEP TOWARD THE NEW YOU!

Now let's take 10 minutes and refine the goals—are there any where you can be more specific or put a target date around it? For example, if you'd like to lose weight—how much and by when? If you'd like to make more money, how much and by what date? If you'd like to retire early, by what date?

Lastly, let's take 10 minutes and prioritize. Which goals are high, medium, and low priorities? Don't worry, we won't delete any of these. In fact, you'll be amazed someday in the future when you see how these impact your subconscious mind! This is just your first attempt at determining where to focus.

BLOCK #2: 30 MINUTES

Turn off your phone. Turn off your laptop. No Facebook, no Twitter, no texting, no Snapchatting. This needs to be solitary time with just you and your thoughts, and you will also need your notes from Block #1 of this exercise.

First 10 minutes: focus on your high-priority goals. For each goal, set outcome and process goals. An outcome goal is the result (I weigh 180 pounds by June 1st 2019). A process goal is an action that will lead you to that outcome goal. For example, I could have two process goals that would support the outcome goal of weighing 180 pounds by June 1st 2019: 1) eat 2200 calories per day in a nutritionist-recommended balance of carbs, fats, and proteins across five meals per day, and 2) exercise five days per week for 30 minutes a day.

Second 10 minutes: For each high-priority goal, determine if you have what you need or if you need to stand on the shoulders of giants (see Chapter 7). Do you need a coach? Do you need a mentor? Do you need an accountability partner? Consider making the goal public, which gives you instant accountability partners. For example, I told my work group I was training for Ironman while I was still 10 months from the race—I knew I had to do it or publicly explain my failure. Failure was no longer an option!

Last 10 minutes: Pick three. In order to get proper focus, you really need to have a handful of manageable goals, not a laundry list. I suggest three. If you want to have four or five, go for it. If you want one or two go for it. I suggest three. Keep the rest—just because you aren't focusing on it today doesn't make it go away. Now, here's the fun part. Look at the supporting process goals and identify three actions you can take right now. Today. Not tomorrow, not next week, not next month. Now. Take action.

CHAPTER 10

PRIORITIZE

"The most important thing is this: to be able at any moment, to sacrifice what you are, for what you will become!"

~Charles Du Bos

EARLY IN MY CAREER, I had a co-worker, friend, and mentor who taught me about corporate America and information technology, but more importantly, he taught me a lot about life. One morning, we sat down to chat and do some training together. He couldn't get through his first sentence without bursting into tears. When I asked what was wrong and how I could help, he taught me the lesson of a lifetime. He said, *"Dave, I've given my life to this place. Late nights. Weekends. So much overtime that kept me away from my family. Yesterday I took my son off to college. I realized I don't even know him. I realized I missed him growing up. I realized I was always so focused on work, evening meetings, and homework that I never engaged with my own family and got to know my son."*

Thankfully, he followed that up with, *"Dave, look me in the eye and promise me you won't eff up your life the way I did mine."* He delivered that message very effectively, and it's always resonated. Because of this experience, I never missed my kids' events—soccer, tee-ball, dance, school events; it didn't matter. As I took both daughters to college, I was grateful that I learned this valuable lesson at an early age and that I'd been able to not just talk the talk, but walk the walk.

IF YOU WANT TO KNOW WHAT A PERSON VALUES, TAKE A LOOK AT THEIR CALENDAR AND THEIR CHECKBOOK

If you want to know what a person values, take a look at their calendar and their checkbook. You'll quickly find out their priorities in life. How do you spend your time? How do you spend your treasure? If you don't spend them purposefully, I promise you they will just slip away.

You have heard expressions like "time flies when you're having fun" at least a thousand times, right? You've had hundreds of days where you were super busy, but at the end of the day feel as if you didn't do anything. Why not? And I know the same holds true for money, right? You look at your W2 and wonder, how on earth did I possibly spend that much money last year? Where did it all go? Time slips away. Money slips away. Unless you plan for it.

TIME + TREASURE + TALENT = YOUR HEART

There's a popular story many of you have heard. It involves a professor teaching a class. When the class began, he wordlessly picked up a very large and empty mayonnaise jar and proceeded to fill it with golf balls. He then asked the students if the jar was full. They agreed that it was. The professor then picked up a box of pebbles and poured them into the jar. He shook the jar lightly. The pebbles rolled into the open areas between the golf balls. He then asked the students again if the jar was full. They agreed it was. The professor next picked up a box of sand and poured it into the jar. Of course, the sand filled up everything else. He asked once more if the jar was full. The students responded with a unanimous "*yes.*" The professor then produced two cups of coffee from under the table and poured the entire contents into the jar, effectively filling the empty space between the sand. The students laughed.

"*Now,*" said the professor as the laughter subsided, "*I want you to recognize that this jar represents your life. The golf balls are the important things—God, your family, your children, your health, your friends and your favorite pas-sions—and if everything else was lost and only they remained, your life would still be full. The pebbles are the other things that matter like your job, your house and your car. The sand is everything else—the small stuff. If you put the sand into the jar first, there is no room for the pebbles or the golf balls. The same goes for life. If you spend all your time and energy on the small stuff you will never have room for the things that are important to you.*

"*Pay attention to the things that are critical to your hap-piness. Play with your children. Spend time with your parents. Visit with grandparents. Take time to get medical checkups. Take your spouse out to dinner. Play another 18. There will always be time to clean the house and fix the disposal. Take care of the golf balls first—the things that really matter. Set your priorities. The rest is just sand.*"

TAKE CARE OF THE THINGS THAT REALLY MATTER

Your priorities are your North Star in life. They should guide your decisions, your actions, where you will spend your time, where you won't spend your time, where you will sacrifice, where you won't sacrifice, and ultimately they will send a message to the world about who you are. Your priorities should be the things you would like to have written or spoken about you when your life is complete. They should reflect your legacy for generations to come. Simply put, your priorities are your story.

YOUR PRIORITIES WILL ULTIMATELY SEND A MESSAGE TO THE WORLD ABOUT WHO YOU ARE

My priorities in life are as follows:

» God—nothing trumps God. My faith comes first.
» Family—aside from God, nothing trumps family. They have always come first and always will. Close friends and loved ones are in the same bucket.
» Health—without health, everything below is irrelevant. Health is an entire lifestyle of nutrition, exercise, sleep, and relaxation.
» Work—I need to provide for my family now and in the future. Hard work is also a sign of character—work hard, play hard.
» Fitness/Ironman—I really enjoy my Ironman training, as long as it enhances and doesn't impede my relationship with God, family time, my health, or work.
» Everything else

YOUR TIME, TALENT, AND TREASURE REFLECT WHO YOU ARE

There's a Bible story that talks about priorities that comes out of the book of Luke, Chapter 10. It says, *"Jesus entered a village. And a woman named Martha welcomed him into her house. And she had a sister called Mary, who sat at the Lord's feet and listened to his teaching. But Martha was distracted with much serving. And she went up to him and said, 'Lord, do you not care that my sister has left me to serve alone? Tell her then to help me.' But the Lord answered her, 'Martha, Martha, you are anxious and troubled about many things, but one thing is necessary. Mary has chosen the good portion, which will not be taken away from her.'*

This story is 2,000 years old, and it speaks to the same challenge that plagues most of us today—priorities. Martha was the multitasker—in our generation she would be busy posting on Facebook that Jesus was at her house, Instagramming pictures of Jesus, cleaning, cooking, and doing pretty much everything except spending time with

Jesus. Mary was the people-person. In our generation, as was 2,000 years ago, she would still be sitting, talking, and just spending time with Jesus.

SET YOUR PRIORITIES. THE REST IS JUST SAND

My mom once told me a story that shaped my perspective and demonstrated to me the value of priorities in our lives. She recalled a time when my father had been laid off. They were not independently wealthy, so this created stress on the family. He provided the sole paycheck, and times were about to get tough. Not once in the story did she talk about the financial challenges of that time. They were there, but she didn't talk about them. She talked about how much the extra time meant to their marriage and how they bonded more closely through adversity and having more quality time together. That's all that mattered, and that's the life lesson she took away. Through crisis comes opportunity. Know your priorities. Live according to your priorities.

My Challenge to You

In the previous chapter, hopefully you took the time to create goals. If not, now would be a great opportunity to go back and try it! Many goals with high priorities, medium priorities, and low priorities. You created outcome (result) goals and process (action step) goals.

Right now I want you to carve out two 10-minute blocks of time. Just 20 minutes of your time! You're on a roll so far; let's keep it going! Turn off your phone. Turn off your laptop. No Facebook, no Twitter, no texting, no Snapchatting. This needs to be solitary time with just you and your thoughts. Have nothing but a pen, paper, and your list of goals from Chapter 9. For your convenience, you can do this in Appendix B—Challenge Journal if you'd like. Or just use your own notebook, or perhaps do it electronically. Regardless of how you do it, just do it.

BLOCK #1: 10 MINUTES

List out your priorities. I shared mine. What's your North Star? What's your legacy? What's your story? What will you and won't you sacrifice? In my priorities, nothing impacts my time with God. God is #1. If Junior's soccer trumps everything, then that's your #1 priority. Make this not a statement of your current state but rather your desired state. Maybe you're in a rut and can't seem to get to church because of Junior's soccer. What do you want to be your #1 priority?

Right now, you need to sacrifice what you are for what you will become.

Okay, now you should have a documented list of your top priorities in life. Look once more. Are you comfortable with them? Do they reflect how you're GOING to start making decisions in life, effective immediately? Do they reflect how you want people to think of you? Do they reflect how you're going to spend your time, talent, and treasure?

Good, congratulations... you're now ahead of about 95% of the general population.

BLOCK #2: 10 MINUTES

Go back to your goals. Especially the high-priority goals. Do they align with your priorities? If God is your #1 priority, do you have goals that support this prioritization? If health is at or near the top of your list, do you have any health goals? Let's take a minute and reevaluate your goals. Maybe reprioritize your goals in the context of your priorities.

If you're getting stuck and having a hard time, maybe you need to sit on this for a day. Sleep on it. Then come back to it. Does your priority list reflect what you truly are becoming? Do you need to create new goals? Now's the time—if you need to take a quick time-out and come up with some new goals or reprioritize, go for it!

Before you go any further, make sure you have a list of priorities and a corresponding set of goals that are in alignment. Nice job!

CHAPTER 11

ORGANIZE FOR EXCELLENCE

"Just get up earlier"

~J. Yusko

IT WAS TIME TO START training for Ironman. One problem—I'm busy! I talked to Coach John about it and put it in the context of my priorities. I said, "God's first. Sunday mornings are consumed with attending and serving at church. Family is next. We have kids at home and at college. I have a busy job that fills up 50 to 60 hours most weeks. Next is health, then work, and THEN comes Ironman. So how do we proceed?"

His answer was unwavering. Just get up earlier. In fact, he asked questions about how much time I spend doing wasted activities like watching TV. How about the hours spent reading and/or posting on social media? Sadly, if you really add it up, most of us have plenty of time every day that could be put to better use. It's all about time management.

I love my sleep. Like most people, I need a minimum of 7–8 hours of good sleep a night in order for my body to recover from the stresses of training and the stresses of life. So back to John's statement, how do I get up earlier?

I figured that if I started going to bed by 9:30, I could get up at 4:30, and that would give me seven hours of sleep while allowing me two hours to train in the morning. This wouldn't interfere with my time with God. It wouldn't interfere with my family time. It wouldn't interfere with my health. It wouldn't interfere with my work. We have a winner.

MANAGE YOUR PRIORITIES, MANAGE YOUR TIME, MANAGE YOUR LIFE

My daughter Tori used to keep a crazy schedule. When she was in middle school, she was taking some hard classes that gave her plenty of homework every night. She was also in competitive dance, which involved quite a few days a week and often started right after school and went up to bedtime. Yes, she was overcommitted, but that's another story.

In that time, she taught me a few things about time management. Most of us think about time in 30- or 60-minute segments. Isn't that what we're taught from an early age? Our favorite TV shows are carved out in segments that are usually 30 or 60 minutes. In school, our classes are carved out into similar segments. As adults, our working calendar is usually broken down into 30-minute segments.

Tori found ways to use those 3–5 minute breaks, those 10-minute breaks, those brief windows of opportunity. She took advantage of every minute of the afternoon. To this day, she's a master of time management and can find time anywhere to get things done.

THERE ARE 86,400 SECONDS IN EVERY DAY—WHAT YOU DO WITH EACH AND EVERY ONE OF THEM IS UP TO YOU

Life is not done in 30-minute blocks. It's done in whatever time is needed. There are 86,400 seconds in every day. The challenge is to figure out how to make the most of those 86,400 seconds. Tell me you have no time to work out—I'll ask you to find 300 of those 86,400 seconds.

Yeah, five minutes. I'm sure you could carve that out. It's a starting point. When you're changing habits, you don't have to start by carving out two hours a day. You start with five minutes and work your way up. Schedule it. Make it part of your day.

You don't have time to prepare healthy meals? Again, let's find a few of those 86,400 seconds. DVR your favorite show, use the commercial time to prepare your food, and then watch it without commercials. Better yet, watch it while preparing food. More and more grocery stores now order curbside pickup—fantastic service! You can literally shop in 10 minutes (only 600 of your 86,400 seconds)! Take the time that saves you and apply those seconds toward preparing meals. Problem solved.

You don't have time for God? This one is so easy. Here's a surprise. God wants a relationship with you—not a bunch of religious acts. In the course of a day, without changing a thing I'm doing, I can easily make a ton of time for God. I can spend several minutes a day in 10-second increments saying things like, "Thank you, God—what a beautiful day." At work I can say things like, "Thank you, God—I appreciate having a job. Please help me to do my job with diligence and integrity." In the evening I can say, "Thank you, God—I have a great family, please bless our time together." Or when challenges arise, "God, I'm scared. This isn't going to be easy. Please help me through this challenge." It doesn't take much. It doesn't require hours of time in church and hours of Bible reading. You can do this.

> *"The key is not to prioritize what's on your schedule, but to schedule your priorities"*
> *~Stephen Covey*

Let's get specific. Let's start with managing time.

Most of us are slaves. Slaves to our calendars. Slaves to our to-do list, and slaves to email, which we allow to become our de facto to-do list. What does your calendar look like? I'm not just talking about your work calendar. Let's talk about your personal calendar. Picture your calendar—one big calendar for both personal and work life—and let me ask, what are your priorities? Your faith? Your spouse? Your family? Your health? Your job? Your other activities? Now, does your calendar reflect those priorities?

Let's play a game here for a minute. Let's pretend your leader has to review and approve your calendar every day. If you are a leader, do not try this at home! It's hypothetical—certainly not a recommended practice. But would your leader think you're spending your time in the most efficient way possible? Or would they look at half the meetings on your calendar and wonder why you're getting sucked into life-draining, useless meetings? Or why you're wasting your time on non-value-add work? I'm going to tell you something that will shock you, but I promise you it's true. I've actually skipped meetings, taken vacation days, and I'm not sure how, but the company stock did NOT drop that day. And so have you. Are you a slave to your calendar? Do you go to meetings just because that's what you do? Or is every meeting an intentional decision that says, "Yes, given my work priorities, this is the best use of my time." Think about it.

Think about this too. What if your spouse/significant other had to approve of your calendar every day? Do you think date night might show up on the calendar more often? Do you think there might be a little less mindless gazing into your phone and surfing email at night? Would they approve how you're spending your time outside the office? What if your calendar had date night on it? What if it had quiet time to talk on it? Then would your spouse/significant other approve? Why aren't those things on your calendar? Why don't you block time off for those activities?

What about your kids? Would they approve of you staring at your laptop every night? My daughter and I used to have a nightly routine that involved 30 minutes of watching *SpongeBob SquarePants* together—no cell phone or laptop allowed. Just quality time laughing together. Do you block off that time to be truly engaged with your kids?

What about church? Is that a game-time decision every Sunday morning? What about community activities, volunteering/service? I bet you have Junior's soccer practices all over your calendar but would never think to put church, service activities, volunteering, or most of these other things on your calendar. I challenge you, start thinking about your calendar differently. Start thinking about what your boss, spouse, kids, God would think of your calendar. Then prioritize it.

CONTROL YOUR TIME OR TIME WILL CONTROL YOU

Sadly, we live in the age of multitasking. The age of smartphones. The age where every app on your phone begs for your attention. Every single email, every single app, every single IM, every single text, every tweet, every single Snapchat is screaming one thing at you, *"I'm the most important thing in your life right now! Drop whatever you're doing and pay attention to me!!!"* It works. I know, I'm guilty too. Unfortunately, that's rarely the best use of my time.

THERE'S NEVER A GOOD TIME TO DO SOMETHING. YOU NEED TO MAKE THE TIME TO MAKE IT HAPPEN

What's the best way to process email? Handle it once, and make one of four decisions: 1) delete it, 2) act upon it, 3) file it, or 4) sit on it only if you plan to act on it within 24 hours. Note that if you're going to file an email that requires follow-up, capture the follow-up action in your to-do list and make a specific reference to the email so you can find it at the appropriate time. Do not be a slave to your inbox, and do not let your inbox drive your priorities.

YOUR FOCUS DETERMINES YOUR FINISH

The best book for organizing your life is called *Getting Things Done* by David Allen. I'd love to spend time talking more about how to organize your to-do list, but I strongly urge you to buy *Getting Things Done* and learn the GTD system. While I'm neither formally trained in GTD nor affiliated with the David Allen Company, I've adopted many of David Allen's techniques and other best-in-class practices because they work!

It's truly amazing to see how much joy you can add to your life simply by organizing yourself and eliminating the clutter that weighs us down. Everything you need to do should be tracked in either your calendar or a to-do list. I personally prefer Toodledo (toodledo.com), as it has many features supported by David Allen's system.

If what you need to do is time-delimited, which means it has a start-time and end-time, put it on your calendar. If it's not bound by a start-time and end-time, put it on your to-do list.

Have one calendar and one to-do list. This calendar should contain everything in your life—work and personal. Maintaining multiple copies for every aspect of your life is not only time consuming, but it's error prone. Most current calendaring and to-do systems have filters that allow you to break out work from personal tasks.

Many to-do tools support productivity features that 99% of the general population has never heard of or used. Let's look at a few of the simpler ones:

» Context: A context simply says, "By what means do I do this?" A context may be something that requires a phone, or it may require driving around. I would call those contexts "phone" or "errand." I have other contexts for things like reading and meeting agenda items, to name a few. Now if I have extended time in the car, I can quickly search on the "phone" context and make some calls while I'm in the car. Hands-free, of course—remember, I was a paramedic. Need to run to Home Depot on a Saturday? Search on the "errands" context to see if there might be some other errands that can be knocked out at the same time.

» Tag: A tag is the most useful feature of Toodledo, in my humble opinion. A tag is simply a person(s) or group related to that task. For example, if my daughter's security deposit for her college housing is due, I'll put "Tori" or "Lexi" (or both) as the tag. This way, whenever I talk to Tori or Lexi, this task will pop up for attention. I also keep tags for groups. For example, if there is a topic I need to discuss

with my leadership team, I'll tag it in Toodledo
with the tag "Leadership Team." Whenever I meet
with them, I filter on the "Leadership Team" tag,
and all of my tasks that apply to the team pop up.
It simplifies the process of creating an agenda, and
it certainly helps keep things organized.

» Priority: How often do you find hours slipping
away as you chip away at low-priority items, only
to leave the high-priority items for last? It's called
procrastination. You did it. I did it. I get it—it
happens. The best use of your time is focused on
the highest priorities. I have recurring tasks for
things I like to do for my wife and kids—topics to
talk about, things to do with them, etc. I even have
questions from a marriage book that I ask my wife
periodically. And yes, they're on my to-do list.
What matters is that you know what your priorities
are and focus on them. I'm not as hung up on how
you label your priorities. I use high, medium, and
low, and that works just fine for me. Some people
like to use a two-level prioritization system: A =
high, B = medium, C = low, and within each category, items are again prioritized as A1, A2, A3, and
so forth... Do what works, but the goal here is to
optimize your time by focusing on the most important tasks first.

» Due date: This is another important item, especially when it comes to filtering. If it's a multi-day
task, then I like to set the due date as when I'm
starting to work on it. By having a due date, it's
easy to filter on today's or other upcoming tasks.
It's also easy to look at the day, and in conjunc-
tion with your calendar, plan your day in advance.
Increases productivity, reduces stress, increases
joy. Simple!

These methods work. They are not mine—I've just
compiled them from a series of best practices. They set
me free, and I want to set you free.

*PEOPLE TEND TO TAKE TIME FOR GRANTED,
AND THEN BEGIN TO REALIZE ITS VALUE AND
IMPORTANCE ONLY WHEN THERE IS HARDLY ANY
LEFT OF IT*

Start using these methods now. It will take you time and patience, so set your expectations ahead of time. Everything inside you will fight change, as it always does, but if you persevere and force yourself to try these disciplines, they will quickly become second nature. I've showed this system to dozens upon dozens of people, and every single one has said it changed their life for the better.

By the way, experts say it takes 21 days before a new behavior becomes habit. In fact, for 21 days, it was brutal waking up every day at 4:30 a.m. to complete my Ironman training. I was never a morning person. Actually, let me restate that. I have never been able to wake up early. I had a self-limiting belief that I couldn't wake up early. I was wrong. It was hard for those first several weeks, no question. After repeating the behavior for 3–4 weeks, it started to become second nature. Now I can say that the wee hours of the morning have been the best-kept secret and have allowed me to do more to be successful than I had ever imagined.

*"Organize your life around your dreams—and
watch them come true"*
~P. Chakraborty

I used to be a slave. To my inbox, my calendar, and my phone. I wasn't the person I wanted to be. I was interrupt-driven and never focused on the right priorities. I never accomplished what I needed until I adopted these practices. Now, my calendar (and yes, checkbook) are very good reflections of who I am and who I want to be.

These tools will unlock the shackles for you. They will set you free, and they will change your life. I pray you never have the conversation I had with my co-worker at the beginning of this chapter—because your time, talent, and treasure will reflect who you are. I want you to be free.

And to be every bit the husband, the wife, the partner, the parent, the person you deserve to be.

This is you taking control of your life. This is you becoming the master of your destiny. Otherwise, do you know what happens? Life. Yep, life happens. Life is busy, life takes time, and life will get you so immersed in the daily grind, the whirlwind, the minutia... you will quickly feel your time and life slipping away.

Do you know why this book is called *Enjoy the Journey*? Because I really and truly want you to enjoy a purpose-filled, joy-filled life of greatness!!! End of story. It's your life. It's your choice. Start right now—take control, live life to the fullest, and just go for it.

My Challenge to You

This is simple, and it doesn't involve taking a quiet time-out with no electronic devices. In fact, for this one you need your calendar and to-do list. The duration is up to you, but it generally takes around 20 minutes.

BLOCK #1: CALENDAR

Look at your calendar. Does it reflect your priorities in life? What would your Creator think of your calendar? What would your spouse think of your calendar? What would your kids think of your calendar? What would your doctor think of your calendar? If you don't like the answers, let's go to work!

Do you work out? Would you like to work out? Start carving out time on your calendar. Daily appointments with yourself, your coach, your trainer... Plan it.

Do you believe in God? Would you like to read the Bible? Pray? There you go—get it on your calendar. It might only be a few 5- or 10-minute meetings, but get them on there. Mark them private if you don't want anyone else to see them.

Do you pre-plan and prepare your meals? Get that time on the calendar.

What about date night, quiet time with your loved one, quality time with your kids? Get it on there! Seriously, if you want to know what a person values, look at their calendar and their checkbook. What are your priorities?

BLOCK #2: TO-DO LIST

We're going to repeat the same exercise. But this time it's on your to-do list—those things that aren't bound by a certain date/time. Do you want to surprise your spouse/significant other with flowers or gifts occasionally? Get it on your to-do list! Do you want to go on a mission trip sometime? Volunteer at a soup kitchen? Volunteer anywhere? Do certain activities with your kids? Get it on your to-do list!

SECTION 5

MAKE IT HAPPEN

CHAPTER 12

BEAR FRUIT

"Girls only want boyfriends who have great skills!"
~Napoleon Dynamite

THE TIRES SCREECHED SO LOUD we jumped... and anxiously waited for about a millisecond. Then the inevitable metal versus metal. A head-on collision at 55 (or more) mph right outside our house. One look out the window at the twisted wreckage, and I knew this wouldn't be good. I had been sitting at home watching an early evening pre-season football game, which was now interrupted by a horrific accident outside my home.

I ran outside. Nobody was out of either vehicle. From where I stood, it was clear that nobody would be getting out of either vehicle soon. One quick shout amongst the bystanders that were quickly gathering at the scene, *"Hey, did anyone think to call 911?"* Thankfully, the answer was yes. Then the waiting... everyone stood around, well-intentioned, wanting to help, and wondering what to do. It was at that point in my young life when I realized something. When I grow up, I want to be a paramedic.

Nobody really cared at that moment that the bystanders were all well-intentioned, good-hearted people who cared. Fact is, we were helpless. We lacked the skills necessary to do anything. The accident victims all wished at that point that just one of us could do something useful to help them. We couldn't.

> *A good tree produces good fruit, and a bad tree produces bad fruit.*
> *~Matthew 7:17*

In the movie *Napoleon Dynamite*, Napoleon made the observation at one point that "*girls only want boyfriends who have great skills.*" What a comical way to teach a valuable life lesson. Yes, girls only want boyfriends with great skills. Want me to let you in on another little secret? Employers only want employees with great skills. If you're a nice person, bonus. If you've got a big heart, volunteer a lot, and are active in your community, that's great. But your employer is hiring you because you have great skills. And in the relationship world, you're being selected because you have great skills.

What have you done for me lately? That's what the world cries out—me, me, me. What can you do for me? What will you do for me? What have you done for me lately? If your answer doesn't involve the use of your great skills, they simply don't care. Period.

Why do you think corporations exist in the first place? They provide products or services that people want or need. They do it to the point where people will pay enough for those products or services that the companies can be profitable. Do companies want people who are nice people, volunteer in their communities, and have big hearts? Absolutely! However, let's suppose two people come to an interview... both are decent people, but one is highly skilled and the other isn't. Guess who gets the job. Easy answer.

Don't get me wrong—if you want to be highly successful and joyful, you need to be an outstanding person, but you also need to bear fruit; to have the skills, knowledge, and abilities to give others what they need.

Let me give you a few words of wisdom, as a manager who has hired hundreds of people in my career. When you're being interviewed for anything and asked to tell about yourself, don't talk about yourself. Get it? Talk about how much value you can add, how you can make a difference, and how much fruit you can bear.

What do you think people want in relationships? Sometimes it's happiness. Sometimes it's companionship or conversation. Sometimes it's physical attraction. Sometimes it's laughter or adventure. Sometimes it's financial. Sometimes it's a partnership. Sometimes it's sharing life's joys and burdens. Sometimes it's spiritual. Most of the time, it's a combination of many reasons. Bottom line, people have needs, and they're asking themselves one question—what can you do for me?

Much like I said above, it's awesome if you're a nice person, you have a great heart, you volunteer/serve, you give to your community, etc. You need those to live a joyful, wildly successful life. But you still need skills, which is the ability to produce fruit and provide what people want or need in life.

How do you bear fruit? Are you smart? Funny? A great listener? Attentive? Supportive? Loving? Kind? A hard worker? Do you know your partner's needs and truly try to bear fruit that meets those needs?

> *"You can have everything you want in life, if you'll just help enough people get what they need"*
>
> ~*Zig Ziglar*

Years after the car accident described above, I went on to get my EMT and then paramedic license. It almost became comical. Hundreds, if not thousands, of calls where bystanders wanted to help so very bad... In fact, people often misrepresented themselves just so they could get in the action and try to help, despite their gross lack of qualifications.

One Sunday morning early in my career, we responded to a possible heart attack in a church. Upon arrival, someone who seemed to have taken charge of the scene met us outside the church. When I asked about the patient, I was promptly told, *"Don't worry, he's in good hands. We've got about seven nurses attending to him."* I wasn't sure if that was good or bad yet, as there are nurses qualified to engage in such a situation, but there are also nurses who have no training or experience in emergency medicine. As I began talking to the patient, all seven of the nurses began talking at once. I finally asked everyone to be quiet, and I asked, "Who here is a registered nurse with emergency medicine experience?" Crickets. I then asked, "Who here is licensed by the state of New York as a nurse at any level?" Again, crickets. Then I had to ask, "Is anyone here really a nurse?" To which they all replied at once, "Yes, we're all church nurses." Again, I appreciated the desire to help, but let's face it, this poor patient was no better off as a result of their care than if everyone had stood back and simply called 911. Nobody could bear fruit.

"For even the Son of Man did not come to be served, but to serve"

~Mark 10:45

The word *servant* is mentioned over 700 times in the Bible. The concept of bearing fruit isn't new—it's over 2,000 years old! The concept of servanthood is simple—you're getting everything you want in life by helping enough people get what they need.

Let's translate that to modern times. I think LeBron James is one of the most fantastic, dynamic athletes of our time. But hypothetically, let's just suppose the Cleveland Cavaliers were to fold tomorrow (sorry, Cleveland, I love you guys, but this example is just too easy to pass up). Do you think that maybe, just maybe, LeBron could get another job playing basketball? Maybe??? And why would he get another job playing basketball? Would it be because he's a great guy who serves and contributes to his community? No. That's part of it. But make no mistake; he would be hired instantly because he bears fruit.

I once listened to Tom Hagan, a missionary, talk about his mission experiences. He summed it up quite simply. He said, *"The best thing you can do, the best fruit you can produce, to change the world is to create a little slice of heaven for someone every day."*

CREATE A LITTLE SLICE OF HEAVEN FOR SOMEONE EVERY DAY

So do it. Do you want to reap rewards like you've never experienced? Do you want to kick your spiritual life into high gear? Do you want to get ahead in your career? Do you want to create an amazing family? Do you want to create a legacy of happiness and a destiny of joy that will last for generations to come? Just do it. Produce fruit. Serve. Live. Love. And create a little slice of heaven for someone every day.

My Challenge to You

Right now I want you to carve out a 10-minute block of time. Just 10 minutes of your time! C'mon, you can do this...

Turn off your phone. Turn off your laptop. No Facebook, no Twitter, no texting, no Snapchatting. This needs to be solitary time with just you and your thoughts. Have nothing but a pen and paper and your priorities. For your convenience, you can do this in Appendix B—Challenge Journal if you'd like. Or just use your own notebook, or perhaps do it electronically. Regardless of how you do it, just do it.

ADD VALUE OR VANISH

Simple question: For each of your priorities, what fruit do you bear? What do you offer? Are you a servant? Are you giving, taking, or both? If the priority is God, then what are you doing for your church? Do you show up, consume their services, and not give back? Or do you serve, volunteer, go on mission trips, and somehow add value? If the priority is family, what are you doing for your family? How do you help your spouse get what he/she wants or needs? How do you help your kids get what they need (besides the obvious outpouring of money)? What fruit are you bearing for them? How are you serving them? If the priority is work, what are you doing for your employer? How are you serving them? Some of you just cringed, didn't you? Don't. I'm going to say it again—how are you serving your employer? What value are you adding? Are you giving your employer more benefit than the salary and benefits you're taking away? If not, you had better rethink this equation. In fact, this is a perfect time to consider what additional fruit you can offer in life so that you're adding more value than you're receiving in your relationships, in your work, and in your life.

CHAPTER 13

OWN IT–BE ACCOUNTABLE!

There are those who make it happen, those who watch it happen, and those who wonder what just happened

Eric Thomas, one of my favorite speakers of all time, tells a story in his *"Secrets to Success"* speech that is a must for anyone who wants to be successful. If you've never listened to him, look him up at www.etinspires.com—I promise you'll be inspired and motivated! He tells of a man who wants to be successful, so he goes to a guru. The guru meets the man at the beach, walks into the water with him, and ultimately holds the man's head underwater until he's about to pass out. As the guru raises the man's head out of the water, the guru says, *"I got a question for you... When you were underwater, what did you want to do?"* The man replies, *"I wanted to breathe."* The guru then says, *"When you want to succeed as bad as you want to breathe, then you will be successful... the only thing you care about when you're trying to breathe is to get some fresh air."*

WHEN YOU WANT TO SUCCEED AS BAD AS YOU WANT TO BREATHE, THEN YOU WILL BE SUCCESSFUL

Burn that visual into your brain. This is the type of focus I'm talking about. Most of us want many things. You already listed those in your priorities and goals, as well as the actions and organization you put around them. This is about the next step… Want. Desire. Focus. Wanting something as bad as you want to breathe. That's what it means to own it. That's what it means to be accountable.

"It's what you do in the dark that puts you in the light"
~TV ad for Under Armour

There are three types of people in this world. Those who make it happen, those who watch it happen, and those who wonder what just happened. The beauty of that truth is that you decide which one you are. Get off the sidelines. Get in the game. Make it happen.

You were born of the seeds of greatness; you were carefully architected with perfection and designed for accomplishment. You were built to fulfill destinies far greater than yourself, far greater than your self-perceived limits, and far greater than most humans ever imagine possible. You were designed to take chances, to live life, to take risks, and to make a difference. Live life to the fullest.

A VISION WITHOUT ACTION IS JUST A DREAM; ACTION WITHOUT VISION IS WASTED ENERGY

About a year ago, my daughter Lexi, a college junior, asked me if she could go on a trip to Europe this year. After some deliberation, I agreed. She gave the obligatory, *"Woohoo, thanks, Dad!"* But then I said, "You can go, but you're paying for it." She said, *"Of course"* in a far less enthusiastic voice.

That day, she created a plan of how many hours she would need to work. She had her outcome goal (result—trip to Europe), and she created the process goals (action steps—work, earn, plan, save). She started focusing on the goal. She turned her dream into action.

For the next year, Lexi picked up hours working at a variety of jobs, and with laserlike focus, she banked money every week. Day by day, week by week, dollar by dollar, she paid off the trip. Day by day, week by week, dollar by dollar, she saved up for her spending money. Along the way, she naturally encountered barriers. Jobs were canceled, hours were cut, she had sick days, and life got in the way. Yet she owned the result and held herself accountable to it. She delivered on her action plan—no excuses! By the way, she is in Europe as I'm writing this, and she's having the experience of a lifetime.

THE KEY IS TO ACCEPT NO EXCUSES. YOU NEED TO OWN IT, FOCUS ON IT, ACT UPON IT, AND EXECUTE ON IT!

My Ironman coach, John, has complete and utter disdain for excuses. After all, Ironman training demands a lot of time, it is physically demanding, and it's mentally on the border of torture. Becoming physically tough requires time—time in the pool, time in the saddle (bike), and time on the road (running). Becoming mentally tough requires exposure to challenging situations—pain, adversity, cold temperatures, hot temperatures, injuries, conflicts with other priorities in life, and pain. Yes, I said pain twice, and for a reason.

As I talked about earlier in the book, coach starts our training at 5:30, which includes a 30-plus-minute drive for most of us. Do you know what happens when my alarm goes off at 4:30? Simple—the first words through my mind are too early, too dark, too cold, too sore from the last workout, too much work. My mind fights me and comes up with every excuse in the book as to why I should hit the snooze. That's when you need to own it. That's when you need to be accountable. That's when you need a trainer, a coach, an accountability partner, to help hold you accountable.

Coach John also pushes us to train through soreness and injuries. I'm currently struggling with a torn rotator cuff (shoulder). He doesn't give me a pass on the pool. Instead, I swim with the team and perform drills using a kickboard. No excuses. Last year I struggled with knee injuries. I didn't get a pass. I modified my training so that if I couldn't run or bike, I swam. No free passes. No excuses. Like the Nike slogan says, *"Just do it!"* Just be smart, and do it safely.

If you're not moving closer to your goal, you're moving farther away. Newton's first law of motion: *An object at rest stays at rest and an object in motion stays in motion with the same speed and in the same direction unless acted upon by an unbalanced force.* Did you ever notice that once you're in the habit of working out, it's easier to keep working out? Once you miss a day or two, and get comfortable not working out, it's suddenly harder to get up and get back to the workouts? Exactly... keep the positive momentum going. Keep moving. Keep growing. Keep learning. Keep getting better. Keep moving closer to your goals. Just keep moving!

BE ACCOUNTABLE FOR YOUR OWN JOY IN LIFE— OWN IT!

I remember a Saturday morning last year, when our team was doing our usual 100-mile ride, I spent some time riding alongside my teammate, Amy. She wasn't having a particularly good day. Amy was a few minutes late that morning, and she got an earful for it from our coach. Clearly this was still weighing on her and had her a bit frazzled. I remember asking her at one point, "Amy, please don't tell me you're giving coach permission to dictate your happiness. Are you???" With a puzzled look on her face, Amy looked over and said, *"Wow, I never thought about it that way. But you're right."*

Have you ever thought about it that way? Have you given permission for others to rob you of your joy? Time to take back control.

Bad things happen in life. They always have. They always will. It's life. Nobody said it would be easy. The challenge is to own the result and stay accountable. Stay accountable to your priorities, stay accountable to your goals, stay accountable to your action plans, stay organized, and focus. *When you want to succeed as bad as you want to breathe, then you will be successful.* Life's not about what happens to you, it's how you handle adversity. It's how you deal with life's challenges. It's how you look at the wall that was dropped in front of you and figure out how to go over, under, around, or through it.

What's your story? What's your legacy? Are you a quitter? Are you a victim? Are you okay looking to your local bartender for sympathy as you tell the story about why you failed? Are you busy pointing fingers? I highly doubt it. If you were, you likely didn't pick up this book in the first place.

ARE YOU GOING TO KEEP LIVING IN THE DAYDREAM OR START LIVING THE DREAM?

There's no room for critics, spectators, and those who stand on the sidelines of life. Watching from the outside in. Not engaging. Not owning it. Not making it happen. Which one are you—one who makes it happen? One who watches it happen? Or one who wonders what happened? Regardless of what you may have been in the past, today is a new day, a new opportunity. Who are you? Effective immediately, you are one who makes it happen. You are accountable. You own results. You accept no excuses. You knock down, go over, go under, or go around any barriers that get in your way.

People engaged with the present, with the people they're with, with the things they're doing, are more productive, happier, and healthier. It's a fact. Do you want to enjoy the journey? Engage. Make it happen. Live life. Take a risk. Go for it. Sadly, I know too many people whose favorite words are shoulda, coulda, mighta, oughta, woulda. Not you. The next chapter of your story starts right now. If the previous chapters were great, then let's make the next chapters even better! If the previous chapters are filled with shoulda, coulda, mighta, oughta, woulda, then let's turn this story around and make it one of no regrets, one of leaving nothing on the table, one of a pattern of successful actions, successful habits, and successful results in all areas of your life.

Act now. Don't wait for something to change. Guess what, the time is now. This is YOUR time. Start today. Start now. No matter where you are. This is your empowering moment. This is your opportunity. This is your ticket to the life you deserve. Go for it, make it happen, and enjoy the journey.

My Challenge to You

Take 10 minutes, no quiet room required, and go back to your priorities, goals, actions, and organizational structures (calendar, to-do list). For your convenience, you can do this in Appendix B—Challenge Journal if you'd like. Or just use your own notebook, or perhaps do it electronically. Regardless of how you do it, just do it.

What barriers are in the way? Where have bad things happened? And you better look in the mirror for this one, but honestly ask yourself, where have you made excuses? Excuses for not accomplishing goals. Excuses for not getting the education you want and deserve. Excuses for your career not being where you wanted it. Excuses for not being involved in your community or service work that you had always planned to do. Excuses for shortcomings on life's bucket list. Excuses for staying in bed instead of working out. Excuses for not spending time with your family. Excuses for a life of shoulda, coulda, woulda, mighta, oughta...

What are you going to do about it? For each barrier or excuse, what action are you going to take to clear the path for success?

CHAPTER 14

REMAIN CALM

It's when people are under stress that true character emerges

I WAS TRAINING A ROOKIE paramedic at one point. We received a call for "an injury." As we calmly pulled up on the scene, we quickly realized this was more than an injury. The blood led from the front door right to the patient, and the patient's hand was a bloody, mangled mess. As we started to work on the patient, I quickly realized there were two patients—my trainee being the second. As my trainee began to work on the patient, the sweat started pouring down his face. From the jitters in his hands, I was guessing his heart rate was through the roof. And then he started projectile vomiting, right then, right there. Both "patients" turned out okay. In fact, my trainee turned out to be a pretty darn good paramedic once he learned to manage stress. However, in that particular moment, stress got the best of him.

STRESS IS THE EQUALIZER—IT SEPARATES THE MEN FROM THE BOYS

It was a Saturday morning when we were called for a man down. Upon arrival we found an elderly gentleman on the ground, not responsive, not breathing. He was in full cardiac arrest—clinically dead. Before I attempted any resuscitation efforts, I asked the family if there was any form of a Do Not Resuscitate order. They said there wasn't and asked me to please do everything possible. Time to get busy... We started working on this man, and after multiple rounds of shocks and drug therapy, we started to get a heartbeat. Within a few minutes, he had a normal heart rhythm, he was breathing on his own, and his vital signs all returned to normal! This, in itself, was nothing short of a miracle. It was a miracle because the patient was in end-stage cancer and had been down for several minutes before we arrived. It was also at that point that another family member showed up on the scene and produced a Do Not Resuscitate order. Yeah... the same Do Not Resuscitate order I had asked for and was told didn't exist.

Our emergency medical system (EMS) had provisions in certain situations where we needed to call special ER physicians who were well versed in our EMS protocols. We could also call them whenever we encountered a rare situation or wanted to provide advance communication. I called the doctor at the ER where we were going to transport this patient. We did our introductions, and I told her I had a hot situation for her. I proceeded to explain the story as listed above. Silence. I asked, "Are you still there?" She said, *"Yes. Did you say the patient was in cardiac arrest?"* I repeated, "Yes, he was in cardiac arrest, isn't anymore, and now a Do Not Resuscitate order has been produced." She commented, *"I've never had someone call in and sound so calm in a cardiac arrest situation. I'll see you in a few minutes."*

I've always viewed my ability to remain calm in stressful situations as critical to my joy and success as a paramedic, as an executive, and in all aspects of my personal life. I've never seen the value in freaking out, and I certainly wouldn't have been able to effectively manage the situation if I were projectile vomiting like the paramedic trainee in the first story. People handle adversity much better when they remain calm, keep a level head, and take a logical approach to resolving the stressful situation. No drama.

One of my favorite business clients of all time, Bob, is a master of managing stressful situations. I remember coming to him with what I felt was a significant problem, and I was expecting to get beat up a bit. As I walked into his office, he must have seen the look on my face, and he knew something was up. He very calmly said, *"Dave, is anyone dead?"* No. *"Dave, is anyone bleeding profusely?"* No. *"Then we will figure this out. What's the problem?"* We calmly sat down together, discussed the problem, talked about the resolution plan, and we then started solving the problem. He never yelled, never freaked out, never lost his cool. His attitude helped drive a faster, more effective resolution than yelling or screaming ever would.

WHEN THE GOING IS GOOD, IT'S EASY TO BE SUCCESSFUL. HOWEVER, IN STRESSFUL TIMES, TRUE CHARACTER EMERGES

Of the millions of qualities I admire in my wife, one of my favorites is her ability to always put things in perspective and to remain calm. With her, there is no drama, no theatrics, no yelling, no irrational behavior. She often says, *"Can you control what happened? If not, then there's no use losing your cool over it."* And if there is, she's one of the most level-headed problem solvers I've ever met. Life's not about what happens to you, it's how you respond. I admire how much joy she has in her life, and I've learned a lot from her. If it doesn't adversely impact life's priorities, if it's not a major detriment to one of your life's goals, and it's not a huge deal in the grand picture of life, why stress about it... let it go.

DON'T SWEAT THE SMALL STUFF—TAKE LIFE IN STRIDE

When bad things happen, how do you respond? Look at how successful people respond. Successful people anticipate and are proactive to avoid bad, stressful situations.

Successful people remain calm and positively respond to stress. Successful people adapt to the situation and figure out what needs to be done.

Compare that to how immature or unsuccessful people handle those situations. Instead of responding, they react. Instead of remaining calm, they flip out, create drama, create theatrics. Instead of adapting, they addict. The easy way out will always be there—drugs, alcohol, running away from your problems. The winners in life tackle the problems calmly, head on.

"Can any one of you by worrying add a single hour to your life?"
~Matthew 6:27

I've been on multiple mission trips to Haiti, the poorest country in the Western Hemisphere. One might think that in a country overrun with poverty, corruption, disease, and a gross lack of food and water, stress would be a problem. I expected to see people stressing out about getting their next meal. After all, wouldn't you expect to see people more stressed out about matters of life and death than a bloody hand? Apparently not. While the people of Haiti live in some of the worst poverty, in which the pursuit of food and clean water is often a daily challenge, they are also the most joyful people I've ever met. Hands down. They've taken control of stress.

"It's not the load that breaks you down, it's the way you carry it"
~Lou Holtz

In the late 1990s, Michael Jordan established himself as one of the best basketball players in history. He was instrumental in driving the Chicago Bulls to six championships in the 1990s. While there have been many great players throughout history, stress is what put Michael Jordan in the upper echelon of his sport. Michael Jordan always asked for the ball when the game was on the line.

Everyone watching the game knew that if Jordan got the ball, he would deliver. Because Michael Jordan thrived on stress. He turned up his game a notch. He succeeded. He dominated. He owned stress.

One thing is for sure, there's stress in life. It's as sure as death and taxes. How you respond to it is up to you. You can be like the rookie paramedic or a multitude of people I've seen who couldn't handle it. You can fail. You can succumb to stress. You can let stress control you. If stress controls you, it will bring you down—in addition to the inevitable health issues, it will destroy your joy.

Or, you can be like Michael Jordan. You can master your own destiny, manage stress, control stress, own stress, and choose your attitude. You can choose to rise above. One life—that's all you've got. You have been given one life, one opportunity to impact the world. Only you can control your destiny, only you can control your future. Now go out there and take back what's rightfully yours, and enjoy the journey.

My Challenge to You

How do you handle stress? Think about it for about 10 minutes. Take out a pen and piece of paper and write down your responses. For your convenience, you can do this in Appendix B—Challenge Journal if you'd like. Or just use your own notebook, or perhaps do it electronically. Regardless of how you do it, just do it. What do you find to be stressful situations? Taking tests? Public speaking? Delivering bad news? Arguments with loved ones? Perceived pressure to do too much with too little time? Inability to get things done? Meetings with your boss? Traffic? Anything else?

How do you respond to these events? Do you feel your heart race? Do you find a lack of clarity in your thinking? Do you get angry? Do you tell everyone how stressed out you are? Do you create unnecessary drama for others? Do you withdraw and avoid the situation? Do you drink, smoke, or use drugs?

Or do you go into planning mode? Do you look for creative solutions to your problems? Do you pray and give your problems to God? Do you focus on keeping a level head and systematically approaching the situation? If you don't know, ask a loved one—hopefully, they'll give you honest feedback based on how they've seen you respond to stress in the past.

Now, how can you improve the situation? Let's start with the basics. Tie it to a priority, if possible. Tie it to an outcome goal, if you have one that fits, or maybe even create a new outcome goal. Now tie action goals to it. I used to get stressed in traffic jams. Now I try to listen to books on CD or listen to Bible readings from my phone. I also try to take alternate routes with less traffic. Maybe you need an accountability partner, a life coach, a mentor who has overcome the same types of stressors you're dealing with. Ask for help. Go back and review Chapter 7: We All Need Help. I used to stress over certain conditions in Ironman training, especially race situations. I've simply learned to put it in the context of my priorities, and I've tied my racing to charity work. Now I'm less stressed about my performance and more consumed with the experience and bearing fruit for others.

CHAPTER 15

FAIL FORWARD

"It ain't about how hard you hit, it's about how hard you can get hit"

~Rocky Balboa

I REMEMBER WATCHING MY CHILDREN as they were learning to walk. They'd try to get up, and they would fall. They tried again. They tried again. They tried again. Somehow, they instinctively knew that eventually they would figure this out. And they did. Then they'd try to take a step, and they'd fall. They tried again. They tried again. They tried again. Somehow, they instinctively knew that eventually they would figure this out. And they did. Then they'd try to put together several steps and actually walk, and they'd fall. They tried again. They tried again. They tried again. Somehow, they instinctively knew that eventually they would figure this out. And they did...

If babies were negatively programmed like most adults, they would never learn to walk. Most of them would never even try to stand up, as they'd be afraid of failure. They'd be afraid to fail, afraid to get laughed at, afraid to not be conforming to the ways of the world. They simply wouldn't try. For those that did try, they would fall once. They'd point a finger and blame their parents, their environment, the carpet, and anything else to justify their failure. Worse yet, they'd try, fall once, and use the "c" word. They'd doom their destiny by saying, "I can't." Not good enough, was never meant to walk, not the right genes, I didn't really want to anyway. And guess what... they'd quit. Never learning to walk, they would quit.

> *"There are no secrets to success. It is the result of preparation, hard work and learning from failure"*
> *~Colin L. Powell*

When I started Ironman training, I couldn't swim. My coach wanted to see what he had to work with, and sadly I told him, "I can't swim." What I should have said was, "I haven't yet learned to swim." I jumped in the water and promptly proved to him that I hadn't yet learned to swim. He said he would teach me. Part of teaching me involved me doing some swims at my local YMCA to practice what I was learning on my own. I'll never forget my first solo swim. I grabbed a lane in the lap pool. I put on my goggles, got ready, and started swimming my laps. I suddenly realized someone in the next lane over was passing me. She couldn't have been 10 years old. And when I say passed, I mean she flew by me like I was standing still. A few minutes later, I realized the same thing was happening on the other side of me. Only this time the woman was considerably older than me. And by older, I won't say elderly, but she wasn't much younger than dirt.

I wanted to hide. I wanted to quit. I wanted to cry. I wanted to make up an excuse and get out of the water and quit. I felt like a total failure. It wasn't so much about the speed (okay, it was a little bit), but I was learning to swim with about as much skill as the five-year-olds taking lessons just two lanes over. I felt humiliated.

Then I heard the voice saying to let go of my ego. Get over yourself. It's not all about you. Fail forward. Thomas Edison, who was considered as a kid to be stupid, once said, *"I didn't fail 1,000 times. The light bulb was an invention with 1,000 steps."* Edison knew that there is no success without failure. Failure is simply learning what will and won't work. Imagine if Edison quit after the 1st attempt, the 3rd attempt, the 999th attempt? Albert Einstein couldn't speak until he was four years old and was also considered to be of below average intelligence. Henry Ford failed and went broke five different times before he became successful. Walt Disney failed and was even fired once for his alleged lack of imagination. Michael Jordan was cut from his high school basketball team. None of them quit—they failed forward. So can you.

THROUGH FAILURE COMES LEARNING, THROUGH LEARNING COMES IMPROVEMENT, THROUGH IMPROVEMENT COMES EXCELLENCE, THROUGH EXCELLENCE COMES LEGACY

One year, I was a featured speaker at the Team Software Process Conference. In that conference, I shared a story of success, but it was also a story of failure. Our organization had embarked on a software engineering quality journey. Over the course of a year, we had some amazing results— speed, quality, throughput, predictability... all the things that technology executives thrive on! We also had some failures. There were some significant shortcomings in the process, and we completely missed a few key areas. On an independent process audit, we were blasted by the auditor in some key areas. The business results were amazing, the technology results were amazing, and most of the executives were thrilled—not the process folks.

We had a choice. Fail backward or fail forward. This team had the right mindset, so we quickly evaluated our toolset and found the cause of our deficiencies. Through failure, we learned. We then made some adjustments. Through learning, comes improvement. We then incorporated the new process and institutionalized it as our new way of working. Through improvement comes excellence. By continuing this pattern, we established a world-class software engineering organization. As you can imagine, our next audit was a huge success, and the business results continued to skyrocket.

Failure is awesome! It's your way of telling the world I haven't yet figured this out. It's your way of telling the world I am getting closer to the solution because I found another approach that won't work. It's a stepping-stone on the way to victory. Failure is a tool. It's an opportunity to learn. It's an opportunity to reassess your approach. It's an opportunity to demonstrate patience, resilience, character, and fortitude. It's an opportunity to set aside your ego, humble yourself, and accept that neither you nor I are perfect. We're human. We're broken. We make mistakes. We're imperfect. And that's okay. While we were in fact wonderfully made and designed for accomplishment, we were also made to fail. The failure, however, was never meant to define us—it was meant to refine us on the way to success.

> *"Fail fast, learn fast, win fast, and win big"*
> *~Scott Howe*

How did my swimming story end? It remains a work in progress. I can tell you that I used a multitude of early failures to grow, improve, and succeed. I have swum over three miles recreationally both in the pool and in open water, and I have successfully raced at the 1.2- and 2.4-mile distances. If I were to jump in that same lane today, flanked on one side by the 10-year-old and the other lane by the "older" woman, how would I do? I would do great. They may or may not be faster, but that wouldn't matter. I've learned that failure isn't measured in comparison to others—it's measured in comparison to myself. And if I want to truly enjoy life, I can't allow my success, my happiness, my destiny to be based on anyone else.

The same holds true for you. Perhaps you're competitive or race against others, and that's okay. Ultimately, you cannot allow their performance to determine your level of success. Okay, if you're an Olympic or professional-level athlete, and your career depends on your ability to place highly amongst others, then you can worry about the competition. However, for the other 99.9% of us, get over it. You certainly can't allow anyone else to dictate your level of joy. It's your life. It's your journey. It's your definition of success. Set your ego aside, embrace failure, use it as a tool by which you can improve, and enjoy the journey.

My Challenge to You

Take five minutes and think about failure. Where in life have you "failed"? How did you respond to that failure? Did it wreck your ego? Did it stop you from enjoying something you might otherwise enjoy? Did it make you feel bad? Or did it help you? Did you use it as a tool? Did you use it as a stepping-stone? Did you allow yourself to fail forward?

Make a commitment to yourself, that much like the baby learning to walk, you will demonstrate that level of resilience. You will accept failure as a natural part of who we are and a healthy tool that helps us grow, develop, and improve. Make it a goal, get an accountability partner, do whatever it takes, but don't allow your joy to be limited because of failure.

Business leaders, how do you handle failure? Do you yell, scream, and berate others? Do you publicly humiliate people and make them feel horrible? Or do you embrace failure as a learning opportunity?

Think about others in your life. Your spouse, your kids, your friends, your loved ones, your teammates, your co-workers... where can you help them use failure as a stepping-stone? How can you help them fail forward? How can you help prevent failure from becoming a crisis but rather enable failure to become an opportunity?

CHAPTER 16

MOVE MOUNTAINS

"Words kill, words give life"
~Proverbs 18:1

MY DAUGHTER LEXI ALWAYS WANTED to be a writer. Ever since 9th grade, she was interested in journalism, and she had every intention of pursuing journalism as a career. As it was time to select colleges, she was looking primarily at schools with great journalism programs. Until... One day she turned in a paper at school, and her teacher asked to talk to her after class. The teacher commented on Lexi's writing and subtly suggested that journalism might not be the best field of study for her. Crushed, Lexi came home and decided to change her life's pursuit.

Ironically, in her freshman year of college, Lexi turned in a paper, and the professor asked to see her after class. Can you guess what he had to say? *"Lexi, you are an amazing writer. Why are you not in our journalism program?"* Go figure.

After much deliberation, soul searching, and praying, Lexi landed on a major that she loves, but she also decided that she would always pursue writing as a hobby. Sometimes crisis is opportunity, so maybe the high school advice was the best thing to ever happen to her and led her down a new path that will open new doors for her. We both believe that God has a plan for us, and we trust *his* plan is the right plan for her. But we will always wonder what might have happened had she continued down the journalism path.

WORDS CAN MOVE MOUNTAINS

In Chapter 3, we talked about the 1980 US Olympic men's hockey team and their insurmountable challenge of playing against the seemingly unbeatable Russian team. The team had already accepted defeat... until Coach Brooks spoke. He said, "*If we played them 10 times they might win 9. But not tonight. NOT tonight. Tonight, we skate with them. We skate with them and we shut them down because WE CAN.*" Words moved mountains that night. Words changed everything. Words gave hope. John Maxwell says, "*When there's hope in the future, there's power in the present.*"

What Brooks did with his words was to give the team hope at a time when things seemed hopeless. His words spoke life into a seemingly dejected and dead team. The result was that the team played the game of a lifetime, and they pulled off one of the biggest upsets in sports history.

> *"Words can inspire. And words can destroy.*
> *Choose yours well"*
> *~Robin Sharma*

Words are a form of programming. Your self-talk is your own way of programming your mind. The words you say to others program their minds, and the words others say to you program your mind. In the Ashanti tribe of Ghana, the practice is to name children based on the day of the week they are born. The boys grow up knowing what their name means—it's just part of the culture.

Boys born on Wednesday are named Quaku, which means violent, aggressive, and quick-tempered. A classic study found that boys born on Wednesday commit over 50% of all crimes in the Ashanti tribe. No surprise, right? Their minds are programmed from the day they're born. Those words program their minds as to how they were supposed to act.

SELF-TALK IS YOUR OWN WAY OF PROGRAMMING YOUR MIND

TobyMac, my favorite musical artist, was interviewed about his song entitled "Speak Life." In this interview, Toby said, *"Anyone we come in contact with... we either offer them life or drain them. There's no neutral exchange... everyone I talk to, I have the chance to offer life to. I can speak life to people and use my words to turn lives around and encourage them, show compassion and love..."* Guess what? We all have that power. Our words can and will change lives. If we choose to speak life, our words will show hope, encouragement, compassion, and love. It's your choice—how will you choose to speak?

> *"We can turn a heart with the words we say...*
> *Speak Life"*
> ~TobyMac

Nowhere have I seen this illustrated better than in the workplace. I once worked with a young man whom we will call Joe. Joe was a great guy, a good friend, and a great worker. At one time, our senior leadership team was stack ranking our organization. Joe's immediate manager put him dead last. She cited her examples of why she felt Joe wasn't very good. While we didn't all agree with her ranking, she convinced enough people, including the senior leader of the group, to rank him very low.

This was Joe's first performance review that wasn't good. Suddenly we all noticed a change in Joe's attitude. He was defeated. He was beat up. He was mentally checked out. The quality of his work suffered as a result. A few organizational shuffles took place, and Joe again found himself reporting to a new manager within the same organization. This new manager started the relationship on one condition—a clean slate with Joe. She didn't support the ranking and didn't want the negative programming to continue to impact his performance. She and Joe then talked... She spoke life into him. Suddenly, Joe had pep in his step. He was rejuvenated, he was renewed, he was alive, and he was thriving. As I'm sure you can guess, Joe's performance skyrocketed. Joe went on to be very successful and was ranked in the top 10% the next year.

In the course of the last 29 years, I've seen Joe's story dozens of times. In each case, it's the words that inspire and the words that destroy. I've watched fantastic workers bottom out because of poor management and a gross failure to speak life, and I've watched struggling workers skyrocket to success because of exceptional leaders who spoke life and truth into their people. In each case, words make all the difference. Speak life.

> *"Be mindful when it comes to your words. A string of some that don't mean much to you, may stick with someone else for a lifetime"*
> *~Rachel Wolchin*

Many of you are like me. You start speaking positive words into your children from the day they're born, and you never stop. Empowering words—you can, you will, I believe in you, you are special, you are loved, you are amazing, you are unique, you are awesome, you have what it takes, I'm proud of you... Sadly, many of us have seen parents who haven't yet realized the power of the spoken word. You've heard them say things like you can't, you're not good enough, you won't, sit down, shut up, don't try it... They see the glass-half-empty side of everything. Don't climb the tree, you'll fall and break your arm.

Let me also caution you. Words you say, even when they're just overheard by others, can move mountains. I remember one time when a friend's child was struggling in school. The child was lacking self-confidence, and it was negatively programming his mind to think he wasn't good enough. One night, my friend was talking on the phone and thought his young son was sleeping. He talked about his son, and in the course of the conversation he talked about how his son is smart, his son is capable, his son can do it, his son has what it takes. Suddenly the boy's grades started getting better. At the next parent-teacher conference, the parents and teachers were asking what happened and what had made the difference. Neither had a clue. After the conference, the parents decided to ask their son what had happened and why he was suddenly doing so much better. His simple reply said it all: *"Dad, I heard you talking on the phone one night, and you kept saying how smart I am and how I can get good grades. I realized that maybe I'm not such an idiot after all."* People hear what you say. Words can move mountains.

How you speak to others programs them for future success... or failure. Speak life... and when you do, you'll feel the joy of knowing that you're empowering and enabling others to become the very best they can be... and that you're changing minds, hearts, and destinies for generations to come.

If you want to experience a more joyful life, don't let anyone else's words steal your joy. It's your life. It's your choice. It's your destiny. Speak life.

My Challenge to You

Take five minutes to think about how you talk to your spouse, your children, your parents, your loved ones, your co-workers, your subordinates, your students, or anyone in your circle of life.

- » Do you speak words of love, encouragement, and empowerment?
- » Do you speak words that will help them become the best they can be?
- » If not, commit to doing it. You will be amazed at what they can do, and you'll be amazed at the power you hold in your words!

Take another five minutes to think about how you receive words.

- » Are you conscious of what messages you're receiving from others?
- » When someone says, "You can't" do you reprogram that message into your mind to say something like "I will"?
- » When someone says you're a failure, do you say, "I simply haven't yet succeeded, but my failure is my tool and stepping-stone to success, which is inevitable"?
- » When someone says you're not good enough, do you say, "I was born of the seeds of greatness, carefully architected with perfection and designed for accomplishment"?
- » When someone says you won't, do you say, "I was built to fulfill destinies far greater than myself, far greater than my self-perceived limits, and far greater than most humans ever imagine possible"?

If not, think about how you're going to reprogram your mind and body for success. Think about how you're going to both send and receive messages that speak life.

CHAPTER 17

BE YOU! BE AWESOME!

"Character is doing the right thing when nobody is looking"

~J.C. Watts

L AST YEAR, MY TEAM DID a bike race called Michigan Mountain Mayhem, which is a 130-mile race on the toughest hills northern Michigan has to offer. At mile 60 I suddenly had issues with my derailleur and I lost the ability to shift. Effectively, I was stuck in one gear, which set the stage for a disastrous final 70 miles. At that point, I was riding alongside my teammate Steve. I looked at him and said, "Steve, just go. I'm really holding you back." Without missing a beat, Steve said, *"No way. We're a team. We stick together."*

This put Steve's time in the tank, as he not only rode slowly with me for the next 30 miles, but he also sat with me on the side of the road while the course mechanics repaired my bike. This move easily cost Steve an hour on his time. Did he care? Not at all. He was focused on doing the right thing. Total class.

CHARACTER IS DEFINED ONE DECISION AT A TIME

Who are you? Who are you? No, I'm not going to start reciting 1970s rock songs. But who are you and what do you stand for? What are you passionate about? What causes would you die for? What defines you as a worker, a parent, a child, a spouse, a friend? We have one shot. That's what we get. One shot at life. One shot to be the best. One shot to make a difference. One shot to leave a legacy of greatness. One shot to dream your dreams and make them come true. So I ask again, who are you?

Few of us dream of mediocrity. How many of you sat in elementary school and dreamed about being average and mediocre? Who wanted an average life, an average job, an average family...? Nobody. We all had dreams of greatness. How are you doing on that dream?

THERE'S A NEVER-ENDING BATTLE IN YOUR MIND: THE RIGHT WAY VERSUS THE EASY WAY

What's the difference between men and boys? Physically I get it. But character-wise, what's the difference? Did you ever notice; boys walk through open doors—men open the doors. Boys say "me first"—men say "after you." Boys are too busy to help—men are always asking how they can help. And yes, you're right, this isn't a question of being an adult male. Being a man is so much more—character, integrity, and putting others first.

Did you ever notice that when you light a candle with another candle, both candles burn just as brightly as the first? That's one of my hopes and prayers for you. That you become a candle. A light. A beacon of hope. A sign of character that shines brightly in the darkness and calls others to emulate you. That your light ignites other candles, so that their light can be seen and their warmth can be felt for generations to come.

THE EASY WAY OUT WILL ALWAYS BE THERE

Some of the greatest failures in history have not been shortcomings in skills, knowledge, or ability. They've been character failures. Consider the sinking of the *Titanic*. Was it that the ship's captain wasn't skilled? No, it was a character flaw that allowed the desire to go fast to supersede his ability to make good, rational decisions for the safety of the passengers and crew. What about the Enron failure? Was it that the leadership wasn't good enough? No, it was a question of greed and a lack of integrity. Near and dear to my heart is the recent bankruptcy of my beloved city, Detroit. Was this just an example of a city that fell on tough times? No. It was a city plagued by years of greed, corruption, lies, deceit, and putting the leaders' needs above the needs of the citizens.

TRUE JOY COMES FROM WITHIN

I often hear parents say, *"I just want my kids to be happy."* I don't. Well, okay, don't get me wrong, I want them to be joyful. Happiness is often just a fleeting feeling, driven by something externally, and it's temporary. Happiness isn't necessarily rooted in who you are. Happiness can even be found in a bottle, a pill, a cigarette, a website, a slot machine…

Joy comes from above, joy comes from within, joy is deeply rooted within you. Joy transcends your current set of circumstances. Yes, I absolutely want my kids to be joyful. I want them to experience this deep-seated state regardless of their circumstances. I want their character to be shaped through life's experiences, and I want them to learn how to manage stress, adversity, and crisis in a positive, joyful manner.

RISE ABOVE!

One of my favorite stories is about a farmer's donkey that fell into a dry well. The animal cried pitifully for hours as the farmer tried to figure out what to do for his poor donkey. Finally, he concluded that the well was too deep, and it really needed to be covered up anyway. Besides, the donkey was old, and it would be a lot of trouble to get him out of the pit. The farmer decided that it was not worth trying to retrieve the animal, so he asked his neighbors to help him fill in the well and bury the donkey.

They all grabbed shovels and began to toss dirt into the well. The donkey immediately realized what was happening, and he began to bray horribly. Crying would be our normal response if somebody was mistreating us this badly, so this donkey was responding the same way we would at first, but then he got real quiet. A few shovel loads of dirt later, the farmer looked down the well and was astonished at what he saw. With every shovel of dirt that hit the donkey's back, the donkey would shake it off and step on top of it.

As the neighbors and the farmer continued to shovel dirt on top of the animal, he continued to shake it off and take a step up. Soon the donkey shook off the last shovel full of dirt, took a step up, and walked right out of the well.

What am I saying? When someone throws dirt on you, instead of seeking vengeance, use the experience to rise above. Vengeance is easy. Forgiveness requires character. Discipline requires character. Be the bigger person. Use it as an experience to mold and shape your character. Rise up, rise above.

"Know that you are unique and special and that the universe is a better place for having you in it"
~Holly Hinton

You were made to be awesome, and you deserve to be awesome. Now take what's rightfully yours. You were uniquely made to serve a multitude of purposes and to make the world a better place. You may be saying, "Who, me?" Yes!!! You!!! I ask again, who are you? Most people answer that question by reciting their job title or saying that they're a student. Come on—really? That's something that you do, but it doesn't define you.

What's your story? Define yourself! And the next time someone asks, "Who are you?" I want you to proudly tell them.

Let's close with five characteristics commonly found amongst highly successful and joyful people:

» *Character*: Character is **integrity** under pressure; if you ever want a test of character, put someone under pressure and see if they crack. It's doing the right things, even when nobody is looking.

» *Charisma*: Most people think charisma is only about magnetic charm. While that's true, it is so much more. Charisma is also the art of getting over yourself—it's not all about you! Before anyone cares how much you know, they want to know how much you care. Start looking for ways to think less about you and more about those around you.

» *Courage*: Courage is being able to make decisions, even when they're unpopular; it's the ability to step out of your comfort zone. Start looking for ways to learn, grow, and push yourself out of your comfort zone.

» *Responsibility*: This is no-excuses accountability: own it, make it happen, and suck it up. When things get tough, get tougher. No excuses.

» *Service*: Service is being a servant to those you lead and giving them every opportunity to be wildly successful. Start figuring out what YOU need to do to make those around you more successful. Whether it be your workgroup, your family, outside organizations, friendships, etc.—how will you enable them? What fruit will you bear?

Being awesome requires action and effort. Ray Lewis says, "*Effort is EVERYTHING, it's between you and you.*" You'll never have to look someone else in the eye and convince them you did your best. However, every day, you have to wake up, look in the mirror, and convince yourself that you've done your best. You've given your all. You've left it all on the table. You know the feeling, when you've given 110%, you're lying on the field exhausted yet exhilarated because you've spent all you could on a worthy cause. That's effort.

Make choices. Look at yourself in the mirror and ask if you're just going through the motions or if you're putting in the effort. Next, write down the choices you're going to make and the actions you're going to take to make your story a reality. Then hold yourself accountable—no excuses. How will you become a person of character, charisma, courage, responsibility, and service?

All choices lead you somewhere—where is up to you. The past is the past. It's behind you. You have in you the seeds of greatness. You were born with the ability to be a great leader and do great things. Fail forward, learn, and make choices starting right now. Make choices that will define you, that will create your legacy that will tell your story. Is it the story of coulda, shoulda, oughta, mighta, woulda? Or will yours be the story of someone who made it happen, who took chances, who got it done, and who made a difference? You may only have one shot, but it's never too late. Grab your dream, make the right choices, live your story, and enjoy the journey.

My Challenge to You

Take five minutes and think about this:

- » I ask the question one last time—who are you?
- » Think about the individuals and groups over whom you have influence—your dominion of influence.
- » Figure out whom you are a role model to? Your kids? Their friends? Your subordinates? Your co-workers? Your outside organizations?
- » Think about how you will exemplify character, charisma, courage, responsibility, and service in your daily life
- » Make a choice about what type of role model you will be and then choose how you're going to get there.

CHAPTER 18

LIVE OPEN-HANDEDLY

"Happiness... consists in giving,
and in serving others"
~Henry Drummond

A S MENTIONED EARLIER, I HAVE been to Haiti several times on mission trips. The first time I went, I expected to see people whose level of happiness was reflective of their level of poverty. I assumed that because the Haitians had minimal food, very limited clean water, minimal education, and practically nothing materially, that they would be sad, dejected, and very lackluster. I could not have been more wrong.

The people of Haiti were the happiest, most joyful, vibrant, dynamic, relational people I've ever met. Their top priorities are God and people, in that order. My Haitian friend Samuel wakes up at 4 a.m. every day so he can have a few hours of uninterrupted time praying before his day really starts. Haitians love spending time with other people, and they really don't care about their lack of material wealth. They've figured out how to enjoy the journey!

"All I ask is your love and friendship—I don't want anything"

~Samuel Cineus

On this first mission trip, I became instant friends with Samuel. Samuel was a local merchant who made a living by selling Haiti trinkets to tourists. His whole net worth was on a small table at the mission. Our last night in Haiti, Samuel asked me to come over to his table, which I expected to be a masterful sales pitch. Instead, he began putting his stuff into a bag for me. Lots of his stuff! I pushed back and tried to stop him. He wouldn't be stopped. He just kept saying, *"You don't get it."* He continued to stuff the bag. I then showed him that I only had a few dollars in my pocket and would pay him for some things but that I couldn't pay for half of what he was giving me. *"This, this is just stuff. But you, you are my brother. I love you."* I then started giving him money, and he was equally adamant, *"No, you don't understand, my brother. I want to do this. This is a gift. I want you to share these things with your American brothers. I want you to pray for Haiti. I want you to have others pray for Haiti. All I ask is your love and friendship—I don't want anything."*

IN THAT VERY INSTANT, LIFE'S PRIORITIES CHANGED

At that particular moment, I was hit over the head with a ton of bricks... Wow... Samuel and I hung out that night and just chatted about life. It was awesome. I eventually said good-bye, got up, and walked back toward our complex. Tears started flowing down my face. Here I was, just now understanding something I hadn't been able to comprehend in my first 43 years of life. It was a complete paradigm shift in my life. I finally realized the value, or lack thereof, of material possessions. My house seemed less significant, my car seemed less significant, my cool electronic gadgets seemed completely insignificant. I also started sponsoring some children in Haiti so they can get food, water, and education. Seems like a much more responsible use of my finances.

Upon returning to the states, I made some major priority shifts in my life, and I began aligning my goals, my time, and my finances with those new priorities. My life was different. It's funny how I went to Haiti expecting to be a blessing to the Haitians and to help them. Instead, the wonderful people of Haiti, including Samuel, proved to be one of the greatest blessings I've ever received.

> *"For those who exalt themselves will be humbled, and those who humble themselves will be exalted"*
> *~Matthew 23:12*

I've always heard that when you give freely of your time, talent, or treasure, what you give is returned to you many times over. Honestly, I had always thought that was a crock. A plot to manipulate people out of their precious time and hard-earned money. I simply didn't buy that whole idea.

Shortly after returning from my first trip to Haiti, I tested that theory. There was a fundraiser for the Hope Water Project, a charitable organization sponsored by Kensington Community Church to bring clean water to the Pokot people of northwest Kenya. It's truly a lifesaving mission, which has become a key part of who I am. In fact, since I've started my Ironman journey, I've used Ironman as an opportunity to raise money and support the Hope Water Project. It also became more personal to me when I started sponsoring two awesome little Pokot girls. We write letters back and forth, and I keep their pictures (as well as my Haiti children) on my desk so that each and every day I'm reminded, on a very personal level, about living open-handedly.

One Sunday morning, I wrote a check for the Hope Water Project. You know, one of those checks where the second it leaves your hand you say, "Oops, I really shouldn't have done that." That night I was wide-awake staring at the ceiling... wondering how I would recover from my own stupidity.

The next day, we got our quarterly bonuses at work, and my bonus ended up being quite a bit more than what I'd calculated it should be. The overage was almost to the penny the same amount I'd written the check for one day prior. Seriously? Seriously! Could this possibly be the weirdest coincidence ever? Maybe. But at this point I was starting to wonder... could this whole silly idea of "giving freely of your time, talent, or treasure" really have a return on investment? No way. I was still skeptical.

And then...

Kensington Community Church had another fundraising initiative. Charlotte and I pledged to give at a certain level, which was over our heads and seemingly impossible. We said to ourselves, "We've stepped out of our comfort zone before and given freely, let's try it again." Again, we were nervous. Would this pattern hold true? Would we really be rewarded for taking this risk? Were we doing something really stupid this time? We weren't sure for a few days, but within a few weeks I received an unexpected bonus as well as a promotion, and within a few more weeks she received both a raise and a bonus that exceeded her expectations. Maybe, just maybe, there's something real about receiving more than what you cheerfully give to others.

I really don't understand it. It's hard to put into words, and unless you have great faith, there's no earthly way to describe it. As much as I've tried to doubt and refute it, I can't. This same exact story has repeated itself at least a dozen times in my life, if not more. It defies logic, it makes no sense, and it's really hard to explain. But it's true... When you live open-handedly and give freely of your time, talent, and treasure, the rewards are unimaginable.

I have some awesome friendships with the incredible people of Haiti. To this day, we write letters and communicate regularly. I sponsor children in both Haiti and Kenya, and we too write letters back and forth. The joy of helping these children have a better life is unbelievable.

Their gratitude jumps off each and every letter, and I feel nothing but love every time I read their letters. Yes, indeed, the rewards are unimaginable.

"When they discover the center of the universe, a lot of people will be disappointed to discover they are not it"

~B. Bailey

C.S. Lewis said, *"Humility is not thinking less of yourself, it is thinking of yourself less."* Giving your time, talent, and treasure is an act of service that says, "I value you enough to put your needs ahead of my own." It takes a big person to do this. Sadly, many people believe that humility requires putting oneself down. It doesn't. Humble people believe in themselves. Humble people have priorities. Humble people have goals. Humble people have amazing resolve to create action plans and achieve their goals in life. Humble people simply have a different perspective that elevates others. Humble people find incredible joy in living open-handedly and giving freely of their time, talent, and treasure to serve others.

Give freely. Live open-handedly. Share the joy. Help others. Live humbly. And reap the rewards. I won't promise you financial abundance, but I will promise you joy. The joy of helping. The joy of changing lives. The joy of fulfilling destinies. The joy of reaping rewards and blessings you can't imagine. Life's a journey, enjoy it.

My Challenge to You

Remember in Chapter 10 when I shared the quote, "*If you want to know what a person values, take a look at their calendar and their checkbook*"? Let's take a look at your calendar and checkbook again, but this time look at it from the perspective of living open-handedly.

Take five minutes to tackle these questions.

- » What percent of your time are you giving to others? Are you volunteering? Mentoring? Coaching? Helping? Serving? Spending time with others in need?
- » What percent of your treasure are you giving to others? What charitable causes are you supporting?
- » Now, think about where you can step out of your comfort zone. What talents do you have that you can share with others? Where can you make time to help others? How can you give financially or materially to help others?

If you're ready to implement change, either add a priority, goal(s), or a task(s) in your to-do list. Make it happen.

CHAPTER 19

LIVE LIFE WITH PASSION

"Not a need to achieve... Instead, a burning desire to exceed all bounds!"
~Dr. Fred Hatfield

IT WAS NEAR MILE 20 of the marathon portion of Ironman Chattanooga when a volunteer looked at me in utter disbelief. As I approached her to take a cup of water, I smiled and "pre-thanked" her for the water and for volunteering. She looked like she had seen a ghost. She said, *"Holy cow, do you even realize you're 138 miles into an Ironman, and you're smiling, laughing, and thanking people?"* Just for the record, Chattanooga for some reason added four miles to the bike course, making it a 144.6-mile Ironman instead of the usual 140.6. Not sure why.

Prior to Ironman, I had set my race goals. Most people set a time goal. Some people aim to simply finish. I had several goals:

1. Enjoy the event.
2. Finish.
3. If I can finish before it gets dark and the race officials make me wear a "glow stick necklace" that would be a bonus.

I truly set out with the intention of enjoying the journey. I laughed. I smiled. I joked with fans. I thanked volunteers. I chatted with other racers. I even met Dan, someone from another Kensington Community Church campus 1,000 miles away! What are the odds?

Ironman isn't supposed to be fun. Ironman brands itself *"the single most difficult day in sports"* and for good reason. Ironman is a race. A grueling test of endurance. But it actually can be fun... with the right mindset, with the right goals and focus, and with a positive attitude, it can be a very fun. If Ironman can be fun, so can almost anything else in life. It's your attitude that makes the difference.

A JOYFUL PERSON IS NOT ONLY JOYFUL IN THE RIGHT CIRCUMSTANCES; THEY ARE TRULY JOYFUL BECAUSE OF THE ATTITUDES THEY'VE CHOSEN

Did you ever wonder how some people just go through the motions of life? How some people always see the glass half empty? How some people always find something to complain about? Do you want me to let you in on a little secret? People don't want to hear what's wrong with you, they want to hear what's right with you.

Two of my closest friends since childhood are people who often have every right in the world to complain. But in the 40 years I've known them, I can't remember either of them ever complaining. That's probably why I have so much love and respect for them.

Craig is the coolest guy you'd ever meet. He has the absolute most magnetic personality you've ever seen. Everywhere we go, people know Craig, and if they don't know Craig they want to know him. He's just a magnet. I've never seen Craig without a smile on his face and an army of friends surrounding him. He's truly an amazing guy. Craig has also had some unfortunate health issues.

He's endured hundreds of painful surgeries. Yet he has never, ever complained. Not once. When you talk to Craig, you would think he's on top of the world. And with an attitude like that, he is! Too many people spend their lives complaining about every ailment they've got. Not Craig. Craig is a role model to me in enjoying the journey.

Kevin is no different. He has a great wife, three wonderful kids, and he is by far the busiest person I've ever met. Kevin can go anywhere and know people. He remembers faces from people in kindergarten, which blows my mind. Never forgets a face, always has something nice to say about everyone, and I've never heard anyone say a bad word about him. Between multiple jobs, constantly coaching his kids in sports, and being completely engaged with the family, he goes 100 mph all the time. Yet every time I call, no matter how busy he is or what challenges he's facing, he never, ever complains. He loves life. He's enjoying the journey. At one point Kevin lost his job, and within a day his basement blew a huge crack. By huge, I'm talking over $10,000 huge. Again, did Kevin complain? No! Was this a burden? Absolutely. But that's just how he rolls—he will tell me what's right with him a hundred times before I ever hear about anything that's wrong with him. Don't get me wrong, we share life's struggles, but it's always done in a positive context. No wonder people love to be around Kevin...

> *"Not a commitment to excellence... Rather, utter disdain for anything less!"*
> *~Dr. Fred Hatfield*

I've often been accused of being an optimist—sometimes to an extreme. I am. There's a reason. Optimism and a positive attitude work together to program your mind for success. Optimism sends loud and clear messages to the subconscious brain at an alarmingly fast rate. The body always moves in the dominant direction of the brain. When your mind is positive and being programmed with optimistic messages, it drives behavior, it drives creativity, it drives problem solving, it drives positive action that delivers the desired outcome.

Let me caveat, if there's a situation over which I have no control, I try to not be quite so optimistic. For example, I'm confident that the Detroit Lions will eventually win the Super Bowl, which they will, but when I watch each game I try to temper my optimism. If I were on the field, I promise you I'd be the most optimistic person out there. Optimism, rather, is the belief that you can positively affect the outcome of any situation such that it will be the best it can possibly be.

> *"Life will hit you in the head with bricks, don't let it stop you. Do what you love and what you believe is great work. Don't settle—you'll know when you find it"*
>
> *~Steve Jobs*

My father used to tell me, *"When you're doing something, don't just go through the motions. Do it! Give it 100%... and when you're not doing something, give it zero percent."* His message was simple: engage. Engage in life. Engage with others. When you're spending time with family, put the phone aside. When you're spending time at work, put the phone aside. Bear fruit in whatever you're doing at that time. If something is important to you, make time for it, but the key is to engage in life and not just go through the motions.

My sister was working on her master's degree at Syracuse University. We lived in upstate NY growing up, and neither of us had ventured too terribly far away for college. One year she visited Denver for spring break. She just connected—Denver, the Rockies, the outdoor life-style, hiking, camping, everyone in Denver loves dogs; everyone is active... It just grew on her, and she realized how passionate she was about Denver. She came home from break, packed up, and moved that same week to Denver. Rather than saying "I can't" or "someday" she took action immediately. Love it...

Natalie, my stepdaughter, is passionate about a few things that naturally go together—music and the city of Detroit. Natalie has been a drummer and vocalist, and she has been involved in several music schools and has worked with some extremely talented music teachers. She loves all aspects of music—listening, playing, and even writing. She's also very interested in the ongoing revival of Detroit. A few years ago, she was trying to figure out how to put these two passions together to make a difference. After a trip to Detroit in which she got a firsthand view of homelessness in Detroit, she decided to produce an all-day concert with many different student and local amateur bands. At the concert, she sold art. Guess what—the art was created by students and local amateur artists. The proceeds all went to a shelter that serves the homeless of Detroit. Passion—when what you love is more important than what you make in the course of doing it.

> *"There is no passion to be found in settling for a life that is less than the one you are capable of living"*
> *~Nelson Mandela*

My friend Bob lives with passion. He too is one of the most charismatic people I've ever met. Everyone wants to be around Bob because they know that Bob brings out the best in everyone. Bob is positive, he's optimistic, he's full of energy, and he loves life. One day out of the blue, Bob looked at me and said, *"Dave, I just love people. People are awesome!"* He thrives on being relational, spending time with people, and really engaging with others.

> *"Success is no accident. It is hard work, perseverance, learning, studying, sacrifice and most of all, love of what you are doing"*
> *~Pele*

Indeed, success is no accident. Going back to my Haiti mission trips, they were some of the most rewarding weeks of my life. I had no laptop, no cell phone, no social media, nothing. I just spent the time "doing life" with my Haitian brothers and sisters. It was fun, it was energizing, it was relaxing, it filled me with purpose and passion. I've always been blessed to have jobs I loved. Sure, there have been challenges and hard times along the way, but there's one thing about every job I've always enjoyed... the people. To me there's nothing like working together with teammates to accomplish things that nobody ever dreamed of. There's nothing like doing the impossible and helping people realize their full potential.

DO WHAT YOU LOVE; LOVE WHAT YOU DO

In addition to my career, one of my passions has always been leading and helping others to levels of greatness they never imagined. I absolutely loved my jobs as a firefighter and paramedic. I absolutely loved my mission trips. I absolutely love serving with my church. I absolutely love my Ironman training. I love those things not because of the mechanics of what I do, but because of the people I've worked with and for. More importantly, I've loved these things because of the opportunities to positively impact the lives of those around me.

If you're in a job or career that doesn't align with your passions, seek opportunities at work to modify what you do to incorporate those passions. Work with your leader to explore opportunities to tweak and/or expand your role. If that's not possible, consider extracurricular experiences (mission trips, volunteer opportunities, part-time jobs) that will allow you to pursue your passions.

Life is too short to go through the motions and spend your time in unworthy causes. You're worth more than that. You're awesome! You deserve a life of joy that's filled with the passionate pursuit of excellence in all you do. You're not getting younger, and time's not going backward. So what are you waiting for??? Start living the life you were meant to live... and enjoy the journey.

My Challenge to You

I want you to make another 20-minute appointment with yourself. Carve out the time, and hold yourself accountable to it. Turn off your phone. Turn off your laptop. No Facebook, no Twitter, no texting, no Snapchatting. This needs to be solitary time with just you and your thoughts. Have nothing but a pen and paper, as well as your list of priorities and goals. For your convenience, you can do this in Appendix B—Challenge Journal if you'd like. Or just use your own notebook, or perhaps do it electronically. Regardless of how you do it, just do it.

Now take a few minutes and ask yourself the following questions:

» Do I live a life filled with passion, or am I just going through the daily motions?
» Do I deliberately take time to truly engage with life and others?
» Do I spend more time telling others what's right with me or what's wrong with me?
» Do I spend too much time complaining about life, or is my passion radiating out of me and positively impacting everyone around me?

Maybe you're finding that you're caught up in the rat race, you aren't pursuing your passions, and you complain more than you thought. If that's the case, no worries; it's easy to do. But let's fix it! Now go back to your priorities and goals, and consider how you should modify them to better incorporate your passions.

Maybe it's not your priorities and goals. Maybe you just need to change your thinking to live a more passionate life. Carve out time for yourself. Relax. Think positively. Laugh. Smile. And enjoy.

CHAPTER 20

LIVE A LIFE THAT EVOKES CURIOSITY

Your life is a message to the world—make yours inspirational!

THE FIRST TIME I MET Alan Willett, he immediately evoked my curiosity. The way he looked at things, the questions he asked, completely reframed the way I thought about things. I liked it. Within minutes, I could tell that he was going places in life. I also knew that I would be going there with him whenever I could.

PEOPLE MAY NOT ALWAYS HEAR WHAT YOU SAY, BUT THEY WILL ALWAYS NOTICE HOW YOU LIVE

You want to change the world? Do you want to inspire others, your co-workers, your children, your family, your friends? Start by living an inspiring life. People may not listen to what you have to say, but they'll almost always notice what you do. Live an inspiring life that will evoke curiosity and set an incredible example for others. Live your life in such a way it causes people to question why... and then tell them.

START BY LIVING AN INSPIRING LIFE THAT EVOKES CURIOSITY

Alan was brought into my organization for the first time nearly 20 years ago. He had one management directive—implement a government standard software development practice. Alan heard and understood the objective, but his approach was radically unique. Alan kept asking, *"Why?"* This drove the manager nuts, in a good way. It forced him to think about the purpose and goal(s) behind the request. Then Alan began talking with the organization, and he was learning to see what the organization was doing well and where we were challenged. In grassroots fashion, he began solving problems from the bottom up, and in the process of this problem solving he was driving employee satisfaction through the roof. Our work processes were becoming easier, our speed and predictability were improving, our quality was improving, and people were working considerably less unplanned overtime. After a little while, the manager started to push very hard for Alan's results.

Alan's response was priceless. *"Ah yes... your process... You would like me to start on that, right?"* The manager emphatically said, *"Yes!"* Alan smiled. Alan looked at him and said, *"It's done. It's done. We solved real-world problems, but in the course of doing so we put everything into the framework to meet your goals."* I've never seen a happier manager—his team was performing better than ever AND had met every business objective.

Alan Willett became president of Oxseeker, Inc. Do you know what the word *oxseeker* means? An oxseeker is a person dedicated to the calm pursuit of excellence and/or a person who consistently inspires the best in others. Indeed, Alan is the ultimate oxseeker.

Alan's approach has always evoked curiosity. Alan has an amazing perspective, and I've never met someone with more repeat customers than him. In fact, I've hired him back several times to consult with several different companies I've worked for. He continues to be a close friend and professional mentor to me. What did Alan's uniqueness do? It evoked my curiosity, it caused me to ask Alan questions, and it has resulted in me hiring Alan many times over. It's also invited Alan to share his story, his life, his beliefs with me, and it's been an incredibly fun and rewarding friendship.

BE BOLD, AND ASK WHY. KEEP ASKING WHY UNTIL YOU FIGURE OUT THE GOAL

As mentioned in Chapter 6, I left a good job at one point to join a small start-up company in the dot-com era. One of the main reasons I took this risk was because of Fred. My friend Bob and I had worked for Fred, and we even called ourselves the founding members of the JLF club, Just Like Fred, as we jokingly hoped to make our entire careers successful on the coattails of Fred's awesome leadership.

Fred was a unique leader. I have never seen anyone with leadership skills like he had. One of Fred's greatest traits was the ability to sit down with any employee at any time, and you would instantly see Fred's desk clear, his computer clear, and his mind clear. There were no distractions. Fred was 100% engaged with and focused on the person in front of him. Eyes, ears, mind, and soul.

Bob and I were only half-joking when we started our imaginary JLF club. We really did want to emulate so many of Fred's interpersonal and leadership behaviors. Why? Because he evoked our curiosity and the curiosity of others. He was unique. He was special. He lived this way not just at work but in his personal life as well. Fred listens like no other, Fred cares like no other, Fred ensures his understanding like no other, and Fred can creatively solve problems like no other. Fred continues to be a friend of mine, and because he dared to be different, that difference is what has led him to an amazingly happy and successful life.

DARE TO TRY, TO MAKE A DIFFERENCE, TO DO THE IMPOSSIBLE, TO FAIL, TO LISTEN TO THE VOICE DEEP WITHIN, TO TRY AGAIN, AND TO GET IT RIGHT

People are bored with conformity. Maybe not in middle school, but in the adult world, people realize the value in uniqueness. How do you dare to be different? How do you dare to add value? How do you dare to take chances? How do you dare to live a life that evokes curiosity? How do you create joy from your uniqueness?

How many people say they want to spend more time with their family? How many live it? How many people say they want to lose weight? How many live it? How many people say they want to exercise? How many live it? How many church-going people want to live their faith? How many live it? How many people want to volunteer and serve? How many live it?

> *"...the fruit of the Spirit is love, joy, peace, forbearance, kindness, goodness, faithfulness, gentleness and self-control"*
> *~Galatians 5:22-23*

What if you lived a life that looked like the fruits of the Spirit? What if your life demonstrated love, joy, peace, forbearance (patience), kindness, goodness, faithfulness, gentleness, and self-control? Can you imagine the people that would be trying to emulate you? Can you imagine how many people would want to know your secrets? Can you imagine what this world would look like? How simple! These are some of the simplest instructions for living, but they're so hard to do. If you don't believe me, just picture the accident on the expressway during rush hour when you have a big meeting with your boss at 8 a.m. Now how's your peace, joy, patience, and self-control doing? It takes something special to live this kind of life, but you have what it takes.

Anyone can say they want to improve, they want to get better, they want to help the world. Very few actually live it. That's why you're reading this book. You can, you will! You're capable of greatness, and you are now equipped to live a life that evokes curiosity.

I love nothing more than when people ask me, what's your story? Sometimes it's about my faith journey. Sometimes it's about my Ironman journey. Sometimes it's about my health and fitness journey. Sometimes it's about my joy. Sometimes it's just because people see something different about me and want to ask, "What's your story?"

Here is my story—I encourage you to create your own!

> *I have broken free of my chains. I have transformed my mind, body, and spirit in a way that has set me free while enabling unprecedented personal joy and success.*
>
> *In 2010, after falling into some unhealthy habits, I found myself facing some health challenges: high blood pressure, high triglycerides, high cholesterol, high sugar, and in a high-risk category for heart disease. More importantly, I was spiritually bankrupt and convinced that the God of the universe could never love someone as messed up as me. I wasn't fulfilling my destiny, and I was in need of a makeover. That's where my journey begins.*
>
> *The transformation was both gradual and sudden at the same time.*
>
> *Today I am a child of Almighty God. I am unique, and I am the only person He created to fulfill my destiny—to positively impact the lives of each and every person I encounter, and that includes you!!! I am a loving husband and father, I am a healthy person, I am a hardworking, exceptional leader, and I am in the best physical shape of my life. I'm purposefully driven to live joyfully and to help others enjoy the journey while becoming greater than they ever imagined possible.*

That's my story. What's yours?

My Challenge to You

This challenge requires you to think for 5 minutes and then write for 5 minutes.

What is it about your story that evokes curiosity? Do you live a life filled with love? With joy? With peace? With patience? With kindness? With goodness? With faithfulness? With gentleness? With self-control?

Do you sense a new priority or goal(s) coming? Do you need an accountability partner(s) to help? Time for some new affirmations on your mirror?

I really want you to spend some time thinking about your life, your story, your uniqueness, and what parts of your story evoke curiosity. What would make your children or grandchildren sit down with you and ask questions about your life? What would make co-workers ask you about your life? What would make friends, neighbors, community members ask you about your life? What would they want to emulate?

Now for your story... do you have a story? Do you have an "elevator speech" you could tell someone in under a minute that would begin to tell your story and hopefully evoke even more curiosity? Let's take 5 minutes, and then you will. Again, use Appendix B—Challenge Journal or your own journal/notebook and write. Write your story, now.

CHAPTER 21

SERVE A GREATER PURPOSE

"And what else is there for me?"

~ Tom Brady

Tom Brady, the legendary quarterback of the New England Patriots, was once interviewed on *60 Minutes*. Brady is considered one of the greatest quarterbacks of all time. He's a four-time Super Bowl champion, he's a three-time Super Bowl MVP, he makes more money in a day than most of us make in a lifetime, he's a celebrity, he was once voted by *Entertainment Tonight* as America's most eligible bachelor, and he's now married to supermodel Gisele Bundchen.

By most standards, he has everything most people would ever dream of. But that's not enough.

In the interview, Brady said, *"Why do I have three Super Bowl rings, and still think there's something greater out there for me? I mean, maybe a lot of people would say, hey man, this is what is. I reached my goal, my dream, my life. Me, I think: God, it's gotta be more than this. I mean this can't be what it's all cracked up to be. I mean I've done it. I'm 27. And what else is there for me?"*

What else is there for me? Are you kidding me? This man seemingly has it all—fame, fortune, success... But he asks, *"What else is there for me?"*

WHAT'S YOUR PURPOSE?

We've talked about your priorities. We've talked about your goals. We've talked about your passions. Hopefully you've been taking the challenges all along, and you now have alignment that ties your passions to your priorities, your priorities to your outcome goals, process goals to your outcome goals, actions to your process goals, and both calendar entries and to-do items to those actions.

Hopefully these questions and exercises have caused you to put things into gear to better understand what makes you tick, what's your passion, what's your purpose.

Now let's go up a level... What's your purpose? This is less about alignment. This is an overarching mission. Tom Brady had thought his purpose was about football, but according to the interview, it wasn't. I've worked out with people for nearly 32 years now who believe that their purpose is in bodybuilding, powerlifting, weight training, running, triathlon, or other sports. I've met people who've put their entire identity and purpose into work. Rarely, if ever, has that ended up being their ultimate purpose.

Guess why. Athletes—you won't always be young and strong. You will slow down, you may become injured, you won't always be in your prime. Workaholics—you will someday retire or become permanently laid off. Then what?

Your purpose can be tied to athletics. It can be tied to work. It can be tied to anything you're passionate about. That's why this is so much fun! I know great athletes who believe their purpose is not just athletic performance but also pouring their athletic knowledge into the next generation by becoming trainers or coaches. I know brilliant workers who believe their purpose is in becoming a consultant or executive coach, which enables them to help others achieve their very best. No matter what the passion, the purpose transcends the individual.

What's yours?

I personally believe that everyone has a God-sized hole in his or her heart. This hole is longing to be filled, and it can't be filled by anything of this earth. That's my purpose. It wasn't always—I found purpose in sports, work, family, friends, partying, and various things at various stages of my life. However, nothing filled it until I began my spiritual journey. Now my purpose is in serving God. This includes positively impacting the lives of others, making a difference, helping others enjoy the journey of life while becoming greater than they ever imagined possible, and living a life that evokes curiosity so that I can be a blessing to others.

Maybe you don't believe that God is your ultimate purpose. I will tell you this unequivocally—regardless of your faith, your purpose is still bigger than you. Maybe it's about making this world a better place, maybe it's about volunteering and serving, maybe it's about positively impacting the lives of others. But ultimately you will find that every successful person, every joyful person, has a purpose in life that goes beyond themselves.

There's more out there. In Chapter 2, I described a near death experience. In my mind, that clearly proved that there's more to life than what we can perceive with our senses. We are all here to serve a greater purpose—the challenge in life is figuring out that purpose and then living it.

> "The two most important days in your life are the day you are born and the day you find out why"
> ~Mark Twain

You are responsible for the journey. It's yours. No excuses. No fingers to point. No blame to assign. You and you alone are accountable for fulfilling your purpose, but first ask yourself, what's your purpose?

My Challenge to You

This isn't a pen and paper exercise. This isn't an exercise of alignment. It's an exercise of the heart and soul. You're welcome to write down your answers, but I really want you to quietly think about these questions for 10 minutes.

What's your purpose?

What's that one overarching thing that future generations will remember you for?

What's that one thing you'd someday want written on your tombstone?

What's the one thing you want people to thank you for when you're on your deathbed?

WHAT WILL IT BE?

» Will it be "Thank you for working so many hours"?
» Will it be "Thank you for running those marathons"?
» Will it be "Thank you for all the time you spent fixing up cars in the garage"?

I think not!

» I hope it's "Thank you for being such a loving spouse and parent."
» I hope it's "Thank you for role modeling the love of God and what it means to be a true follower of Jesus."
» I hope it's "Thank you for living the fruits of the Spirit and demonstrating love, joy, peace, patience, kindness, goodness, faithfulness, gentleness, and self-control.
» I hope it's "Thank you for positively impacting the lives of others and changing the world."
» I hope it's "Thank you for teaching me to believe in myself and helping me be greater than I ever imagined possible."

» I hope it's "Thank you for daring to make a difference."
» I hope it's "Thank you for teaching me to be amazing but also taking time out to enjoy life."

The choice is yours—what's your purpose?

BE THE
TOP 3%

CHAPTER 22

WIN!

"Run in such a way as to get the prize"
~ 1 Corinthians 9:24

In 1999 I RAN MY first marathon in Buffalo, NY. The location is only significant because it was late spring, and all of my long runs had been done on cool (55-60 degree) days. This particular day was over 75 degrees, and it was humid. It was humid except for a slight breeze that picked up various scents from the zoo and drifted them across the course at about mile 23. Given my state of dehydration, the heat, and the natural exhaustion that hits somewhere between mile 18 and 22, the smell of zoo animals sent my stomach into convulsions.

However, I finished a few minutes later. I finished something that seemed impossible just a year earlier. I had changed my paradigm.

When I got home, my three- and four-year-old daughters asked the natural question, *"Did you win, Daddy?"* I confidently and honestly answered them, "Yes, I did."

I didn't win my age group. I didn't win the overall race. Based on the race results, I didn't even come close to placing. But in my mind, I had won.

YOU'RE THE JUDGE AND JURY; ONLY YOU CAN DEFINE WHAT WINNING IS

At the Chattanooga Ironman, three of us sat together in the morning waiting to jump into the Tennessee River to start the race. I looked at my coach and said, "Wow, this is impressive. Look at the company we're in. There are some really lean, ripped, elite athletes." Coach John's reply floored me. *"Dave, you haven't figured this out yet, but you are now one of those lean, ripped, elite athletes."* My paradigm changed.

I don't walk around claiming to be an elite athlete; I'm not. However, after losing so much weight and reducing my body fat as far as I did, it took a while to even recognize myself in pictures.

Perhaps the greatest part of that race was in the last two miles. I was having fun. I was engaged with spectators. I was laughing. Every camera that took a picture of me on the course, whether I knew it or not, caught me smiling. It wasn't a coincidence. In mile 142 I'm not sure that would have been the case. As I made one turn, after over 11 hours of racing, the fans lining the streets in their lawn chairs all stood up and gave me a standing ovation. It was at that moment I realized I was about to become an Ironman. It was at that moment that I realized that Jesus had carried me despite my knee that wasn't capable of running 26.2 miles after racing for nearly seven hours. It was at that moment that I declared victory. As tears streamed down my face, I realized I had won.

Again, I didn't place. I didn't expect to. I didn't even finish in the top tier of athletes. But in my mind, I won.

WINNING IS...

Winning is when you have no ceiling. It's when you are free from the chains that bind you to mediocrity. It's when your mind, soul, and body realize that you're in charge of your destiny. It's when you live with character, honesty, integrity, charisma, courage, responsibility, and service. Not because you have to, but because of who you choose to be. It's when you're focused on a purpose higher than yourself, you have priorities in life that align with your purpose, your goals are all focused on your priorities, and your daily actions are focused on your goals, that ultimately feed up to your purpose. Winning is when you treat everyone around you with love and respect. Winning is when everyone wants to interview you—not because you're a Hollywood celebrity but because you're a star in the game of life.

Winning is whatever you define it to be, based on your purpose, priorities, and goals. And your definition of winning can change at any time, including now. What will it take to win? What's your strategy? What's your game plan? Guess what... You've already got it.

When I did a lot of powerlifting, I realized something. No matter how much I could lift, there was always someone else who could lift more.

When I did a lot of bodybuilding, I realized something. No matter how big or cut I was, there was always someone else who was bigger.

When I do my triathlon training, I realize something. No matter how fast I am, there is always someone else who is faster.

Does this mean I've lost? No. My success, my definition of victory, is not tied to what others can or can't do. It's tied to me. And once I learned that I'm only competing against myself, my level of joy skyrocketed. I'm in complete control of the game—it's me versus me.

GRAB YOUR DREAM AND THEN BELIEVE IT

Dr. Dennis Waitley said, "*It doesn't matter if you've won before. It makes no difference the halftime score. It's never over until the final gun. If there were one. So keep on trying and you'll find you've won. You grab your dream and then believe it. Go out and work, and you'll achieve it.*"

Legendary football coach Vince Lombardi said, "*Practice does not make perfect. Only perfect practice makes perfect.*"

He would know. Everything the guy did was 110%. 110% mentally—focused on form, technique, learning, studying, preparing, pre-playing future victory, replaying past victory. 110% physically—pushed, pushed, and pushed until there was nothing left to push. Winning isn't just a game time attitude, it's what we do every day. Every day matters. Every action matters. Every minute matters.

"Kid, you'll move mountains"

~Dr. Seuss

Today is your day. Do you realize that today is the only day that truly exists? Tomorrow doesn't exist yet. It's a futuristic concept that we've come to rely on, and yet we constantly postpone what we can do today until "tomorrow." Why? Make it happen. Today! I challenge you, today, to consider the Goliaths in your life. Make a list, write them down, and then write down your win strategy. How are you going to attack them? How are you going to leverage what's on the inside of you, to win? How are you going to rise up and above and defeat the enemy? What priorities do you need to set, what goals do you need to define, what actions do you need to take? Enough is enough... Stop allowing Goliath to steal your joy. Take it. Own it. Make it happen. And enjoy the journey.

Dr. Fred Hatfield says, *"If you believe these things, then for you winning is neither everything nor the only thing. It's a foregone conclusion! But, if along the way, you should somehow stumble, profit from the experience! And vow, by the power of Almighty God, it'll NEVER happen again!"*

My Challenge to You

Take 5 minutes and think...

What is winning for you? For many people, it's achievement of their stated purpose. For others, it's achievement of their stated purpose, accomplishment of their biggest goals, and living in alignment with their priorities.

This is your story. At the end of your life, if someone asks you if your life was a success, what would it take for you to say, "*Absolutely—my life was a huge success!*" Think about it for a few minutes, and write it down. This is your destiny.

If it's not aligned with your purpose, priorities, goals, or actions, let's go back and adjust those at this time.

CHAPTER 23

PUTTING IT TOGETHER

Make your story one for generations to come

Victor changed his paradigm—everything changed. The US Olympic hockey team believed—everything changed. Roger removed the self-perceived limits—everything changed. Now it's your turn... time to change!

In Chapter 9, we talked about the fact that the most successful 3% of our population has documented, current, relevant goals that shape how they eat, sleep, and breathe. I hope you have taken the time to do that. Here's another chance. Let's recap a few key points that will help you not only hit that top 3% but do so while living a purpose-filled, joy-filled life.

Your purpose drives your priorities, your priorities drive your outcome goals, your outcome goals drive your process goals, your process goals drive your actions, your calendar entries and to-do items are how your actions get focus. If you want joy in life, it's time to focus on living a life of joy. Stop wasting your time, talent, and treasure on things that don't matter. This is your roadmap to living a life greater than you could ever imagine and enjoying the journey.

YOU WERE DESIGNED TO MAKE A DIFFERENCE

To be successful, you need a winning attitude. This starts with realizing who you are and where you come from. You aren't one in a million but rather one in over 7.2 billion! You were born of the seeds of greatness, you were carefully architected with perfection and designed for accomplishment. You were built to fulfill destinies far greater than yourself, far greater than your self-perceived limits, and far greater than most humans ever imagine possible. You were designed to take chances, to live life, to take risks, and to make a difference.

Understand that life's not just about a destination, but it's also about the journey to that destination. Stop saying, "Thank God it's Friday." Stop saying, "I can't wait until..." And start saying, "Thank God it's today." Better yet, take the words "I can't" out of your vocabulary right now. Completely.

Believe in yourself, believe in miracles, and believe in the impossible. After all, you are one of the greatest miracles in the history of the earth. Think about that... You. Yes, you. You, in fact, are an amazing miracle—a one-in-7.2-billion miracle. Now act like it! For a miracle like you who was born of the seeds of greatness, there are no limits. If you think you can, you can. Believe in yourself! Believe in others, and tell them. When some-one believes in you, accept it—they probably have a good reason that you can't see or understand yet!

LEARN IT, LIVE IT, AND LOVE IT!

Crisis is opportunity. There are no bad experiences. Life's not about what happens to you, it's how you respond. Ask for help. We were meant to live in com-munity—help each other and accept help! We're human, we're imperfect, and we're broken. Face it. If you think anyone else is perfect, hand them an award for best actor or actress. They're not! We all need help, and sometimes the greatest demonstration of strength is falling on your knees acknowledging and asking for help.

Evaluate your priorities, goals, and actions often! I look at mine at least once a month. Things change, especially our perspectives and our problem-solving skills. What's not clear to you today may emerge with great clarity next month. The low-priority goal last month may now be more important. Continue pursuing your passion, continue following your dreams, passionately pursue your purpose, and continue making those subtle course corrections along the way. However you define winning, you can and will do it!

Remember, no excuses. It's your life. It can be a pathetic story to your local bartender about shoulda, coulda, woulda, mighta, oughta. Your bartender may commiserate with you, but that's not the legacy you want to leave. No blame, no excuses, and accept full accountability. Make your story one for the ages... for generations to come. Master your destiny.

You will fail, you will hit rough patches, you will fall down, and when you do, get up! Remember, if babies quit as soon as they tried to walk and failed, every adult would be crawling around on all fours still. Get back up and try again. Fail. We all do. It doesn't mean you're a failure, it simply means you haven't yet succeeded. Don't let it define you—you are so much more than that.

You're awesome. You're amazing. You can. You will. Now live that way! Rise up, rise above, and live with class. Live with character. Live with integrity. Live with honesty. Live with charisma. Live with courage. Live with responsibility. Live a life of service. Live the fruits of the Spirit. Live a life that evokes curiosity. Live open-handedly. Live a life that makes people want to emulate your amazingly unique qualities. And live it with passion.

REAP A DESTINY

Stephen Covey says, "*Sow a thought, reap an action; sow an action, reap a habit; sow a habit, reap a character; sow a character, reap a destiny.*" I hope that this book has got you thinking. I hope that this book has started the actions. Repeated actions are what will turn the actions into habit.

Continue the habit and you'll have the character. If you live with this type of character, I assure you, you will reap a destiny that will fulfill your purpose. And along the way, enjoy the journey.

My Challenge to You

For 10 minutes, let's think about your future.

Let's pretend your life is a movie that's being filmed right now. Only one thing—you can't edit what's happened up until this point. You can only use it to create a better ending. You just wrote the ending in your last challenge. Now let's expand upon it. What does that ending look like? Who are the main characters in the next chapters? How will the plot twist and turn? How will the setting change? What will be the outcome? How will you transform your current situation into the victory you described in the previous chapter?

Only you can write the final script. Now get busy—take 10 minutes and write the screenplay. Lights. Camera. Action...

CHAPTER 24

ENJOYING THE JOURNEY

I can. I will. I'm good enough. I can do all things. I can make a difference. I can change the world

IUSED TO LIVE MY life in chains. Not literally, but I was bound and limited by myself. My self-perception. My self-limiting beliefs. My paradigm. My lack of priorities. My impotent goals. My lack of focus and action on what's truly important. My fear—fear of failure, fear of success. My inability to live first for God, then for others, and lastly for me. My inability to live open-handedly. My inability to win. And ultimately, my inability to enjoy the journey.

I was too focused on the destination, and yet I was too distracted by the daily whirlwind that consumes all of us. Everything in my life screamed for time and attention—phone calls, emails, texts, social media, smartphone notifications, and more. Yet those things weren't necessarily aligned with my priorities, and I was losing valuable time, talent, and treasure along the way. More importantly, I was losing valuable joy.

> *"So you are no longer a slave,*
> *but God's child"*
> *~Galatians 4:7*

My chains are broken. You've heard my story. My purpose set me free, and with the right mindset and the right approach, I've been able to do a 180 in my life. I've been set free. Now, I'm setting you free—showing you the light, the hope, the opportunity to live the life you were meant to live, and the ability to create the destiny you were meant to fulfill.

What's your story? I'm not asking about your past story—that's behind you, and you can't change that. You can, however, define the rest of your story from this point on. Starting this second. Everything that happens for the rest of your life, starting right now, is up to you. It's your story. Create it, live it, tell it...

> *"Then you will know the truth,*
> *and the truth will set you free"*
> *~John 8:32*

Life's not meant to be watched from the sidelines. Get in the game. Live. Take chances. Have fun. Fail. Theodore Roosevelt once said, *"It is not the critic who counts; not the man who points out how the strong man stumbles, or where the doer of deeds could have done them better. The credit belongs to the man who is actually in the arena, whose face is marred by dust and sweat and blood; who strives valiantly; who errs, who comes short again and again, because there is no effort without error and shortcoming; but who does actually strive to do the deeds; who knows great enthusiasms, the great devotions; who spends himself in a worthy cause; who at the best knows in the end the triumph of high achievement, and who at the worst, if he fails, at least fails while daring greatly, so that his place shall never be with those cold and timid souls who neither know victory nor defeat."*

Thank you for being with me in the arena. For striving with me to do the deeds. For spending ourselves in a worthy cause.

"Life should not be a journey to the grave
with the intention of arriving safely in an
attractive and well-preserved body.
Rather, skid in sideways with
chocolate in one hand, a latte in the other, body
thoroughly used up, totally worn out,
and screaming
'Woohoo, what a ride!'"
~Paul Mozak

Charles Schulz once asked a set of six questions:

» *Name the five wealthiest people in the world.*
» *Name the last five Heisman trophy winners.*
» *Name the last five winners of the Miss America contest.*
» *Name ten people who have won the Nobel or Pulitzer prize.*
» *Name the last half dozen Academy Award winners for best actor and actress.*
» *Name the last decade's worth of World Series winners.*

HE THEN ASKED ANOTHER SET OF SIX QUESTIONS:

» *List a few teachers who aided your journey through school.*
» *Name three friends who have helped you through a difficult time.*
» *Name five people who have taught you something worthwhile.*
» *Think of a few people who have made you feel appreciated and special.*
» *Think of five people you enjoy spending time with.*
» *Name half a dozen heroes whose stories have inspired you.*

The message is simple. Serve a higher purpose. We're not here for fame, fortune, or celebrity status. We're here to serve God, serve others, and enjoy the journey.

> *"Joy is a deeper emotion that is connected with well-being, living a life of meaning, and living according to values"*
>
> *~LaRae Quy*

Look in the mirror. Do you want a better world? Start with a better you. Not a single one of us can eradicate world hunger. Not a single one of us can eradicate poverty. Not a single one of us can provide clean water to the world. Not a single one of us can educate all of the uneducated. However, we can all make a difference. We can all do something. And together, we could all do everything. Make a difference.

> *A young man is walking along the ocean and sees a beach on which thousands and thousands of starfish have washed ashore. Further along he sees an old man, walking slowly and stooping often, picking up one starfish after another and tossing each one gently into the ocean. "Why are you throwing starfish into the ocean?" he asks. "Because the sun is up and the tide is going out and if I don't throw them further in they will die." "But, old man, don't you realize there are miles and miles of beach and starfish all along it! You can't possibly save them all, you can't even save one-tenth of them. In fact, even if you work all day, your efforts won't make any difference at all." The old man listened calmly and then bent down to pick up another starfish and threw it into the sea. "It made a difference to that one."*

Think you can't change the world? Think you can't leave a lasting legacy? Think you can't create a destiny that will change minds, hearts, and lives for generations to come? Think again. Create a slice of heaven for someone else each and every day.

You can. You will.

YOU ARE THE ONLY ONE WHO CAN CONTROL YOUR FATE, YOUR LEGACY, YOUR DESTINY

It's up to you. I challenge you to dream big. Dream big with no boundaries, no restrictions, no self-imposed limitations. Then act. You can do this. Isn't this what your life is really all about??? Change minds, change hearts, change lives, change your destiny...

Your biggest enemies are the voices in your head that cast fear, uncertainty, and doubt. The more you act, and the more you start to make a difference, the more they will try scream out "You can't." That's when you listen instead to the voice of dissension... the voice that says you can, you will, you are...

LIVE LIFE ON YOUR TERMS, THE WAY YOU WANT TO, THE WAY YOU WERE MEANT TO BE

I close by again quoting Myles Munroe: "*The wealthiest place in the world is the cemetery... there is buried the greatest treasure of untapped potential.*" Don't let your potential go to the grave. You were born of the seeds of greatness, you were carefully architected with perfection and designed for accomplishment. You were built to fulfill destinies far greater than yourself, far greater than your self-perceived limits, and far greater than most humans ever imagine possible. You were designed to take chances, to live life, to take risks, and to make a difference. Live life to the fullest... And just go for it. I promise you the journey of a lifetime that you won't regret.

Enjoy the journey,

Dave

APPENDIX A

CHALLENGE SUMMARY

Chapter	Challenge Summary	Est. Duration	Date Complete
1 – One in a Million	Think about what makes you unique	5 min	
2 – Life's a Journey	Think about your purpose, destiny	5 min	
3 – Believe in Miracles	Think about miracle-like circumstances	5 min	
4 – Believe in Yourself	Think about where you do/don't believe in yourself	5 min	
5 – No Limits	Write down your false, self-limiting beliefs	10 min	

6 – Embrace Crisis	Think about adversity in your life	5 min	
7 – We All Need Help	Write down how you're going to pursue others who can help you through challenges	10 min	
8 – Change the Paradigm	Write down your affirmations	20 min	
9 – Aim High	Write down and modify your goals	60 min	
10 – Prioritize	Write down your priorities and align them with your goals	20 min	
11 – Organize for Excellence	Update your calendar and to-do list	20 min	
12 – Bear Fruit	Write down how you add value	10 min	
13 – Own It – Be Accountable	Identify and respond to barriers	10 min	
14 – Remain Calm	Write down how you respond to stress and how you can improve	10 min	
15 – Fail Forward	Think about your approach to failure situations	5 min	
16 – Move Mountains	Think about your choices when it comes to the words you speak and hear	10 min	

17 – Be You! Be Awesome!	Think about the type of person you are and who you're becoming	5 min	
18 – Live Open-Handedly	Think about how open-handedly you live with your time, talent, and treasure	5 min	
19 – Live Life with Passion	Think about how passionately you live your life	20 min	
20 – Live a Life that Evokes Curiosity	Write your story	10 min	
21 – Serve a Greater Purpose	Think about your purpose in life	10 min	
22 – Win!	Define what winning means to you	5 min	
23 – Putting It Together	Write the next chapters of your story	10 min	

APPENDIX B

CHALLENGE JOURNAL

FOR EACH CHALLENGE, REFER TO the chapter for the full challenge.

CHAPTER 1 ONE IN A MILLION

Think about what makes you unique

CHAPTER 2   LIFE'S A JOURNEY

Think about your purpose, destiny

CHAPTER 3   BELIEVE IN MIRACLES

Think about miracle-like circumstances

CHAPTER 4 BELIEVE IN YOURSELF

Think about where you do/don't believe in yourself

Chapter 5   No Limits

Write down your false, self-limiting beliefs

CHAPTER 6   EMBRACE CRISIS

Think about adversity in your life

CHAPTER 7   WE ALL NEED HELP

Write down how you're going to pursue others who can help
you through challenges

CHAPTER 8   CHANGE THE PARADIGM

Write down your affirmations

CHAPTER 9 AIM HIGH

Write down and modify your goals

CHAPTER 10   PRIORITIZE

Write down your priorities and align them with your goals

CHAPTER 11   ORGANIZE FOR EXCELLENCE

Update your calendar and to-do list (use the space below for notes; otherwise do the exercise in your calendar and to-do list)

CHAPTER 12   BEAR FRUIT

Write down how you add value

CHAPTER 13   OWN IT – BE ACCOUNTABLE

Identify and respond to barriers

CHAPTER 14   REMAIN CALM

Write down how you respond to stress and how you can improve

CHAPTER 15   FAIL FORWARD

Think about your approach to failure situations

CHAPTER 16 MOVE MOUNTAINS

Think about your choices when it comes to the words you speak and hear

CHAPTER 17   BE YOU! BE AWESOME!

Think about the type of person you are and who you're becoming

CHAPTER 18   LIVE OPEN-HANDEDLY

Think about how open-handedly you live with your time,
talent, and treasure

CHAPTER 19 LIVE LIFE WITH PASSION

Think about how passionately you live your life

CHAPTER 20   LIVE A LIFE THAT EVOKES CURIOSITY

Write your story

CHAPTER 21   SERVE A GREATER PURPOSE

Think about your purpose in life

CHAPTER 22   WIN!

Define what winning means to you

CHAPTER 23   PUTTING IT TOGETHER

Write the next chapters of your story

ABOUT THE AUTHOR

Dave VanEpps is a marketing technology executive, Ironman and marathoner, missionary, former firefighter/paramedic, husband, father, and child of God.

His journey began when he was spiritually bankrupt, grossly overweight and unhealthy, and needed help.

In the course of his journey, Dave has done life amongst the richest and the poorest. He's seen people at life's best and life's worst. He's studied how people respond to life under stress, and he's captured the essence of what drives success and failure. More importantly, he's figured out and will share with you what enables people, regardless of their circumstance, to enjoy the journey of life.

The ideas in this book are simple, straightforward, and achievable. They just require the right mindset and the right execution. You deserve to live an abundant life filled with success and happiness. The tools and ideas in this book will help you take what's rightfully yours.

Dave did it. So can you.

Enjoy the Journey, LLC
Motivate. Inspire. Transform.

Mr. VanEpps has a full schedule with limited availability for speaking engagements and events. To learn more about Dave's availability, programs, packages, and pricing, or to contact Dave for any reason, please reach out via:

 www.DaveVanEpps.com

EnjoyTheJourney@yahoo.com

 @DEVanepps